D0422158

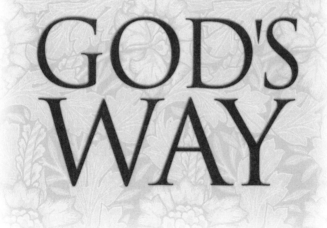

# MOTHERS
## LIVING A LIFE OF FULFILLMENT...

# GOD'S WAY

WHITE STONE BOOKS
LAKELAND, FLORIDA

07 06 05 04 03          10 9 8 7 6 5 4 3 2

*MOTHERS - LIVING A LIFE OF FULFILLMENT...GOD'S WAY*
ISBN 1-59379-005-8
COPYRIGHT © 2003 JOHN M. THURBER
THURBER CREATIVE SERVICES, INC.
TULSA, OKLAHOMA

EDITORIAL DEVELOPMENT AND LITERARY REPRESENTATION BY
MARK GILROY COMMUNICATIONS, INC.
6528 E. 101ST STREET, SUITE 416
TULSA, OKLAHOMA 74133-6754

EDITORIAL MANAGER: CHRISTY STERNER

PUBLISHED BY WHITE STONE BOOKS, INC.
P.O. BOX 2835
LAKELAND, FLORIDA 33806

# INTRODUCTION

*He has made His wonderful works to be remembered.*
PSALM 111:4

God is faithfully at work today in the lives of people around the world—revealing His ways, demonstrating His power, and expressing His infinite love. Do you know that He wants to do the same for you?

Are you looking for answers to the many questions you deal with as a woman?

Do you need a generous helping of encouragement to help you handle the challenges of your life? Perhaps you are facing pressures in a career, in raising children, or in building a family. Do you need a touch from God to succeed with grace and poise?

Maybe you simply need a reminder of how God is at work in the world changing lives today—including yours.

*God's Way for Women* is filled with true, personal stories that present spiritual insights from women experiencing the same range of life situations you face; from women who have looked to God for help and hope—and received it.

Prepare to encounter new levels of power and grace in your life as you experience what it means to live a life of purpose...*God's Way.*

# CONTENTS

A Thankful Heart ❧ *Nanette Thorsen-Snipes* ............................11

I Raised an Angel and a Devil ❧ *Gwendolyn Mitchell Diaz* ....15

A Child of Our Own ❧ *Kathryn Lay* ..................................21

Treasures of the Heart ❧ *Nanette Thorsen-Snipes* ..............27

Right Where I Want to Be ❧ *Wendy Dunham* ..............................31

Hospital Maneuvers ❧ *Betty Winslow* ..................................35

The Cost of Loving ❧ *Linda Rondeau* ..................................43

I Love You, Caitlin ❧ *Stephanie Jacobs* ..........................49

My Little Man ❧ *Lena Hunt Mabra* ......................................57

Given to God ❧ *Linda Henson* ............................................61

The Mirror ❧ *Linda Henson* ................................................67

The Ideal Family That Wasn't ❧ *Sharon Hinck* ..........................73

A New Beginning ❧ *Pat Sellers* ........................................79

Timmy's Ring ❧ *Nancy C. Anderson* ....................................87

A Good Day ❧ *Heidi Sanders* ..............................................93

Out Loud ❧ *Laura L. Smith* ................................................97

Miracle on a Sunday Afternoon ❧ *LaRose Karr* ....................105

A Little Reassurance ❧ *Wendy Dunham* ..........................109

The Richest Family at Church ❧ *Sally Ann Smith* ....................113

Lord, Bring Her a Christian Friend
    ❧ *Susanne Scheppmann* ............................................119

Dancing to a Different Tune ❧ *Kathryn Lay* ..............................123

Be Not Afraid ❧ *Staci Stallings* ........................................129

God Put a Song on My Lips ❧ *Nancy Gibbs* ....................133

The Birthday ❧ *Karen Majoris-Garrison* ....................................137

NOTHING IS TOO HARD FOR GOD ❧ *Joan Clayton* ...........................143

FORGIVING OUR PRODIGAL SON
   ❧ *Nanette Thorsen-Snipes* ....................................149

I COULDN'T LET GO OF MY CHILDREN,
   SO THEY LET GO OF ME ❧ *Joan Clayton* ...........................155

MOTHER KNOWS BEST ❧ *Jennifer Johnson* ....................................161

PICTURE OF A HOME ❧ *Judy Briggs* ....................................169

MIRACLE IN THE RAIN ❧ *Jan Coleman* ....................................173

COURAGE ❧ *Gloria Cassity Stargel* ....................................181

ROCK MUSIC, ROCKY, AND RACHMANINOFF
   ❧ *Susan Jennings* ....................................189

THE LITTLE RED WAGON ❧ *Patricia Lorenz* ....................................193

IT WAS A GOD THING ❧ *Teresa Griggs* ....................................199

THE HUMBUG HOLIDAYS AND THE LEAN-TO SNOWMAN
   ❧ *Patricia Lorenz* ....................................203

OUT OF THE DARKNESS ❧ *Tonna Canfield* ....................................209

APPLE PIECES OF RESTORED LOVE ❧ *Kathy Collard-Miller* .........213

THE LORD'S LULLABIES ❧ *Melinda Lancaster* ....................................219

ABCS AND SLEEPLESS NIGHTS ❧ *Marlene Bagnull* ....................................223

NOT SO SMART AFTER ALL ❧ *Pennie Bixler* ....................................229

GIVE HIM UP ❧ *Cathleen A. Poulsen* ....................................235

THE HARE-RAISING EAR INCIDENT ❧ *Todd and Jedd Hafer* ........241

RIGHTS AND PERMISSIONS ....................................246

MEET THE CONTRIBUTORS ....................................249

TELL US YOUR STORY ....................................255

# MOTHERS
## LIVING A LIFE OF FULFILLMENT...

# GOD'S
# WAY

# THANKFUL HEART

## NANETTE THORSEN-SNIPES

*He said unto me, "My grace is sufficient for thee: for my strength is made perfect in weakness." Most gladly therefore will I rather glory in my infirmities, that the power of Christ may rest upon me.*

2 CORINTHIANS 12:9

The day was supposed to be a day set aside for gratitude—Thanksgiving. But this cool November day with the wind whistling outside, I was less than thankful. I fished another boiled egg from the pot, and as I began shelling, I could feel the angry heat rush to my cheeks. My husband had helped me start the turkey, then squirreled himself away on the sofa.

"Do you need any help?" my husband asked as he peered from behind the sports page.

"No," I answered tersely. I tossed the half-peeled egg into the pan. I could feel the tears building, and I fought the feelings of self-pity beginning inside me. I picked up the hospital bracelet my daughter had just taken off and threw it in the trash.

Just two days before, I had rushed my teenage daughter, Jamie, to the emergency room. For nine long hours, I stood beside my daughter wondering what caused the severe pains in her stomach. The emergency room doctor poked, prodded, and tested my daughter as she continued to double over in pain, often retching into a plastic pan.

One by one, the doctor ruled out ulcers, kidney problems, a stomach virus, and a pelvic infection. About mid-day, I felt relieved to see our family doctor. He gingerly felt her abdomen causing her to shrink from his hand. I noticed he kept coming back to her right side, watching her reaction. Finally, he stepped back and told me he thought it was her appendix.

By 9:00 P.M., Jamie had her inflamed appendix removed. While her problem had disappeared on the operating table, mine had just begun.

I had hoped the bustling activities of the Thanksgiving holiday at my oldest son's house would keep me busy—so busy I wouldn't remember that Thanksgiving was the time of year my former husband, my boys' father, had chosen to commit suicide. But now, with my daughter's surgery having just occurred, Jamie would be unable to make the trip to my son's. And the memory would linger at the edge of my mind.

I stood at the kitchen sink, my head pounding. A lone tear trailed my face. I dialed my next-door neighbor, Donna. "Do you have any aspirin?" I asked, trying to keep my voice from quivering.

"No, but I'll be glad to pick up some for you," she said cheerily, indicating she had to go out anyway.

I sighed. "That's all right. I really need to get out." My voice cracked a bit and I added, "This is just not a good day for me." I hung up the phone. Nothing had gone right. Thanksgiving? What a joke. I was incapable of being thankful for anything.

I drove alone to the store, my nose still red from crying. I felt so exhausted, so tired. I wondered how I would ever make this small Thanksgiving come together for my husband and two teenage kids.

I could feel myself becoming wrapped up in self-pity with my energy level hitting rock bottom. By the time I drove back to my house, I felt so weak I just wanted to crawl in bed.

Pulling into the carport, I noticed a little pot of gaily wrapped lavender flowers beside my back door. *Jamie is so loved,* I thought. My daughter's friends had shown up all week with flowers, teddy bears, and videos. I brought the flowers inside and set them on the table.

To my surprise, the simple white piece of paper in the flowerpot had my name on it. "His strength is perfect when our strength is gone," the card read. As I turned it over, I realized it was from my neighbor, Donna, who was busy with a large family gathering. The heaviness in my heart began to lift. Of course, I thought, my neighbor was right.

I touched the soft lavender petals, considering how thoughtless I'd been. Right there, I whispered, *"Thank You, Lord, for a neighbor like Donna who cares enough to give me flowers to heal my heart."*

I'm grateful that when I can't get beyond my own self-pity, God in His infinite wisdom, provides a neighborly act of kindness to get me back on the right path.

When I returned to my pot of eggs, my husband stood by my side, shelling them with me. The smell of the roasting turkey filled the room. He placed his arm around me and kissed my cheek. And my heart overflowed with gratitude.

# *I* RAISED AN ANGEL AND A DEVIL

## GWENDOLYN MITCHELL DIAZ

*All hard work brings a profit, but mere talk leads only to poverty.*

PROVERBS 14:23 NIV

I was trudging through a department store with several toddlers in tow when I spotted a big red plastic bat with a large white Wiffle ball attached. I recognized immediately that this combination could provide hours of backyard pleasure for my children and become the perfect pastime to fill their long summer afternoons. The fact that it was only $2.99 cinched the decision. I bought it.

As soon as I pulled into the driveway, all of my little boys jumped out of the car, grabbed their new paraphernalia, and headed straight for the backyard. Immediately they started staking out the bases, displaying an incredible depth of knowledge about a game I had never even known them to observe. Picnic benches were moved and boundaries were established. The orange tree was foul, the birdbath was fair, and a home run had to sail over the clothesline. And then the games began.

Before long, paths between the bases had carved themselves into the backyard grass. I spent endless hours pitching to eager batters and reminding youngsters which way to run to first base. One afternoon I found myself flat on my back, staring at the clouds after having been bashed in the head by a hard-hit Wiffle ball. It was our first indication that Matthew might one day be a slugger. And Zach, who had convinced us that he was a "lefty," soon began striking me out with two well-placed fast balls and a funky curve.

Once the boys had mastered all the backyard basics I had to offer, Dad was incorporated into the process. Over the next few years he taught each one of our sons how to stand in the batter's box, grip a change-up, and take a secondary lead off first base. He spent endless hours hitting fungos, evaluating curve balls, raking clay, and driving vanloads of high-school boys to faraway fields.

No matter how much we gave them, the boys always wanted more baseball. They quickly moved from Wiffle ball games in the backyard to Saturday T-ball tournaments at the city field with their buddies. They begged us to sign them up for Little League teams and wouldn't think of missing a single practice. They invited classmates over to watch the "Cubbies" on TV and celebrated birthdays with their teammates at Marchant Stadium.

I realized that baseball had become an obsession when we spent an entire three-week family vacation visiting all the major league ballparks within driving distance. After the trip, my boys could tell you all about the teams that played on each field and could even point out the highest-paid hitters and the wiliest pitchers on each team. I, on the other hand, could only tell you where to get the best bratwurst (Milwaukee); which team has the best organist (Chicago White Sox); and where not to use the restrooms (Boston—not one toilet would flush the day we visited Fenway!).

As they entered their high school years, my sons began spending early mornings in the weight room and late afternoons running long distances around the lake. By this point, most of their buddies, friends, and teammates had dropped out of the baseball scene. For my boys, it wasn't all fun and games anymore, and I often wondered when their enthusiasm would flag. There were many other activities they had to miss and lots of cold meals waiting for them at home. But they kept insisting on working hard to improve their strengths and compensate for their weaknesses. They've each had to overcome injuries, discouragement, uncooperative college schedules, or various coaches' idiosyncrasies in order to keep playing the game; but the results have been astonishing.

This summer a scout from the Tampa Bay Devil Rays showed up on our front doorstep and signed Matthew to a professional contract as a power-hitting outfielder. A few days later we received a call from the Anaheim Angels who needed a left-handed pitcher in their bullpen. Who knows how much longer each of them will choose to stay in the game? But what had started out as a $2.99 impulse buy at the department store turned into a life-changing investment.

As parents, we got them started and taught them a little about baseball along the way. But our kids have taught us major lessons about determination, perseverance, and how to enjoy the gifts God gives. They have each invested a lot of time and energy in the sport, but they've also received a lot of compensation for their dedication.

Baseball has taken them across the country and even to Africa, where Zach participated on a summer "Athletes in Action" baseball team. They have had many outstanding experiences, received college scholarships, made new friends, and had countless opportunities to share their faith.

And me? I've had the unique privilege of raising an "Angel" and a "Devil"!

*Thank You, Lord, for the lessons You constantly teach me*

*through my children. Their perseverance and diligence in developing the talents You have given them inspire me. It encourages me to be dedicated and industrious in my role as a parent. It prods me to persist when my tasks seem overwhelming. Teach me to value hard work more than trite pleasures; to toil more than I talk. Give me a persevering heart, dear God, one that delights in the talents of my children and sticks to the tasks You assign.*

# $\mathscr{A}$ CHILD OF OUR OWN

## KATHRYN LAY

*He who promised is faithful.*

HEBREWS 10:23 NIV

Michael or Michelle.

Even before Richard and I married, we agreed that this would be the name of our first child. We had it all planned. Two years after our wedding, my husband would finish his degree and we would have a baby.

We talked about our three kids, a boy and a girl, then one we'd adopt. I knew Richard would be the best father in the world, and I hoped I'd be the kind of mother whom my children adored.

In two years, Richard walked across the stage to receive his diploma. Yet, ten years later we were still waiting for our second dream to be fulfilled.

It was a decade of roller-coaster rides through a false pregnancy, infertility tests, and watching enviously as our friends and siblings had their first, second, and even third children. My heart ached with jealousy as I forced smiles and joyous responses when they talked of their childrens' accomplishments.

"Will it happen this time?" I'd ask my husband as I took yet another pregnancy test. Pacing and praying, I waited while the moments dragged by until I could look at the results.

Negative. They were always the same. No matter how much I tried to pretend the test could be defective, I knew the dream had escaped us again.

We plunged into our work—Richard into his teaching and me into writing. We talked of adoption but worried over finances, long waits, and family acceptance issues. Yet, our desire for a child was stronger than these worries, and in August 1990, we attended an orientation class for adoptive parents.

I worried all that day before we went, fearful that somehow we'd "fail" at this too, that somehow we wouldn't be acceptable or desirable as future parents.

We were one couple of many streaming into the small room. I looked around the crowded room of nervous couples who clasped hands tightly and smiled when talk turned to adoption. I wondered if our dream could really come true, if someday soon a little girl or boy would truly call us Mom and Dad.

I was afraid to hope. I thought back to a time, eight years

earlier, when the doctor gave us the news that I was pregnant. After spending six weeks preparing a nursery, shopping, and planning, our dream became a nightmare as I discovered that my desire to become pregnant had been strong enough to make my body believe it was true. As we stored away the baby items we'd purchased, I lost hope.

But now we were trying again, a different road toward the same desire.

"This is our chance," Richard whispered while we read through the information packet.

We were invited to begin ten required parenting classes. They would be tough, we were told. The children were coming from broken homes and would need lots of attention. But I was ready to work for the family we'd longed to have.

Every Monday evening for ten weeks, we listened, role-played, and discussed the joys and trials of parenting these children who needed new homes. Our class of eight couples had soon knitted together in a common goal.

The paperwork was unbelievable. Richard and I learned much about ourselves, our childhood, and our goals and beliefs as future parents, many things we'd never thought of before. When our caseworker began home visits and personal interviews, I again fought crushing fears that we would be turned down for some reason.

Yet, with all the work came the joy of preparation and the excited anticipation. How long after we completed our classes and were approved would our child or children arrive? We'd asked for either one or a sibling group of two children. Would we get a boy or girl, or maybe one of each? Would he or she come with a broken heart or a wounded spirit? How long would it take to bond with our child and he with us?

Together Richard and I prepared our extra bedroom. Would it be a nursery or child's room? Did we need a crib or a bed, or maybe even both? There were so many plans to make, yet so little information to help us with those plans. Lovingly, I placed bottles of lotion and powders beside bibs and books inside dresser drawers.

On a bright day in August our final approval came. We celebrated at a favorite restaurant and feverishly completed painting and cleaning the bedroom. Often, I would sit on the floor in the yellow-and-white room and dream of the child who would soon sleep and play there. I even found myself purchasing a few toys and stuffed animals. They waited quietly in the room for small hands to hold them.

As Halloween drew near, I found myself crying as I had so many holidays before. We were told that children were rarely removed from foster homes into adoptive families during the Thanksgiving and Christmas seasons.

But then, on November 4, 1991, the phone rang and our lives were changed.

"Kathy, is there something you've been wanting for Christmas?" our caseworker asked.

I could almost hear her smiling. I clutched the phone and whispered, "Yes."

"Well, I've got some good news."

She began telling me the statistics of an eight-month-old girl. A baby girl! Would I wake and find it just another dream?

"You can pick up her file in the morning. If you like what you've read, next week you will meet with the foster parents, caseworkers, and supervisors," she explained.

"Her name is Theresa Michelle."

Michelle! Although a middle name, it was the name we'd chosen over twelve years before.

As I read the file, I tried to imagine what it would be like to hold this child. We would not see the baby until we agreed that what we had read about her was truly what we were seeking.

Within a week, we had given our answer of "yes," and three days of visitation with our new daughter began.

"My children had trouble saying the name Theresa, so we've always called her Michelle," her foster mother explained.

I looked into my daughter's face. She smiled and held her arms out. I held her and breathed in the scent of baby powder and milk, as sweet smelling as a garden of roses.

Our Michelle had arrived.

On Saturday, November 23, she came to live in our home and in our hearts. Every day our love for her grows. Soon she will be a teenager, and each year she grows in her independence. As I look back on the three children we'd dreamed of, the two from our own bodies and one through adoption, I see how we were blessed with the child of our heart.

Hopes and dreams don't have to die. We watched ours come back to life and call us Mom and Dad.

# 𝒯REASURES OF THE HEART

## NANETTE THORSEN-SNIPES

*...Mary treasured up all these things and pondered them in her heart.*

LUKE 2:19 NIV

"Not again," I said as my husband, Jim, brought in another scrawny tree. *Next year,* I thought, I want a tree like the one in Macy's—with delicate pink bows peeking from the branches and slender ribbons cascading like miniature waterfalls.

I sighed as I watched my children, Jamie and Jon, lug boxes of ornaments from the basement. Before I even touched the first box, I dreaded taking out the faded chains of construction paper and other odds and ends we'd collected over the years. Within minutes, the kids began hanging the bright, red and blue balls and stringing the silver garland on the tree. My mind wandered back to the beautiful tree dressed in dazzling pink at Macy's.

"Come on, Mom, let's hang the ornaments," said Jamie.

Reluctantly, I sat on the floor beside my daughter and peered into the box. "Look!" she cried. "This ornament says 'Baby's First Christmas'." Her blue eyes sparkled with excitement as she added, "It has my name on it!"

As she hung it near the top of the tree, I remembered her birth. My only girl among three boys, she had been special from the start. Immediately following her birth, I recalled cradling her against my body, touching her soft, sweet-smelling fingers, and kissing her forehead.

In the quiet of that moment another birth came to mind. That baby was special too. I'm sure His mother counted His toes and fingers, kissing each one. I can almost imagine her soft voice as she cooed to Him, cradling Him in her lap. I'm sure she kissed his forehead and whispered His precious name—"Jesus".

My eight-year-old's voice broke through my reverie. "Mom, this is my star!" he said. I smiled as I took the tin star from Jon's hand. It was not so long ago when his father helped him patiently hammer his name across the front. As I stood to hang the star, I thought of the Star of Bethlehem that had led the wise men to the birthplace of the Son of God. I could scarcely imagine the brilliance of that star announcing the greatest birth the world has ever known.

Jim handed me an angel with lace wings. "Who gave you

this?" he asked.

"Barbara," I said softly. My thoughts raced back to another year when my good friend and I exchanged gifts after a disagreement. As we sat across from each other in the restaurant that week before Christmas, I made uneasy small talk. And, as we had for many years, we exchanged our gifts. Just before I was ready to leave, my friend hugged me as though no cross words had ever been spoken, as if nothing had ever happened.

As I drove home that day, an inner joy had spread through me. I smiled as I realized that what we had really exchanged that day was the gift of forgiveness. What greater gift could friends give to one another?

I placed the angel ornament near the top of our tree. Long ago an angel had appeared to an unassuming group of shepherds, bringing the news of great joy to all people—the humble birth of the baby Jesus. Ironically, this baby—the very Son of God Himself—would one day die a cruel death on a tree, as He prayed, "Father, forgive them, for they do not know what they are doing." I bowed my head, thanking my Father for allowing forgiveness to take place.

My breath caught in my throat as I realized that for almost every ornament I hung, an equally important event had taken place in the life of my family. Our lives were symbolically hung on that scrawny Christmas tree. Until that moment, I'd never noticed how precious the timeworn ornaments had become.

Looking back, I now can see how much the love of God was embodied in a simple ornament given to a baby, a tin star made by a child and his father, and an angel with lace wings given in love by a friend.

# RIGHT WHERE I WANT TO BE

## WENDY DUNHAM

*He settles the barren woman in her home as a happy*

*mother of children.  Praise the LORD.*

PSALM 113:9 NIV

Forget the movies and fine dining on a Saturday night— I was at home and having fun.  My daughter, Erin, had just transformed our bathroom into a beauty parlor and could hardly wait to begin my makeover.

I watched Erin as she strategically arranged her "makeup" and Barbie cologne on our vanity.  She had chosen deep orchid lipstick (purple), peony nail polish (neon pink), lavender eye shadow (with sparkles of course), and bright pink blush (the words bubble-gum flash might have been more accurate!).

As she lavishly applied the purple lipstick, Erin stepped back and said, "Mom, you look so great!"  Then, with all her six-year-old sincerity, she looked at me as if I were the most beautiful woman in the world. And for those few moments, I believed I was. With her tiny doll comb, she "fixed" my hair so it was completely flat against my head, and then she placed her plastic pearls around my neck. "Wait here, Mom," she said, "I'll be right back." She soon returned with earrings. "I've picked just the right ones," she assured me and displayed my jingle-bell earrings in her palm. Being six, she didn't care that Christmas was already four months past.

Next, she brought in my wedding shoes; it had been eleven years since I'd stepped into them. As she slipped them on my feet, I was Cinderella at last. It wasn't long, however, before my feet were numb and my toes tingled—ankle socks and fallen arches left little room for comfort. But I kept them on, for we hadn't yet had our dance.

For the finishing touch, Erin tied two scarves together for a shawl and placed them over my shoulders. "There, Mom," she said. "You're gorgeous!"

When we finally danced our dance, that night I was the most beautiful (and the most blessed) mother in the whole world. My grown-up soul had been restored with the joy, hope, and wonder of a child. And as we waltzed through our living room, I couldn't help but think, *This is right where I want to be.*

Sometimes being a mom can get downright overwhelming—there are so many responsibilities and so little time for yourself! But one thing I've found that helps me get through the difficult times, is to keep a journal to remind myself of all the times when being a mom is such a blessing.

Keep track of all the wonderful ways God works in your life as a mother, and of all the ways your children bring blessings to you. And the next time you're feeling a little overwhelmed, take out your journal, find a quiet place to sit (I know there's one out there somewhere!), and then read through your past entries. There will be so many blessings to remember, you'll surely be renewed!

# HOSPITAL MANEUVERS

## BETTY WINSLOW

*The LORD is near to all who call on Him, to all who call on him in truth.*

PSALM 145:18 NIV

In 1990, our daughter, Lisa, received an appointment to the U.S. Naval Academy, and our family joined the ranks of military families throughout the ages, waiting by the phone, haunting the mailbox, living from one military leave to the next. When Lisa volunteered to be one of twenty midshipmen sent to sea during the waning days of Desert Storm, she was beside herself with excitement, but the rest of us spent the whole time praying for her safety and hoping that no uniformed stranger would knock on our door with the news no one wants to hear.

To our joy, she returned home without a scratch, filled with stories about navigating uncharted minefields, working on a ship stocked with explosives, and sightseeing in a foreign country. But she was home, and she'd be safe from now on. We heaved a sigh of relief.

But, on a cold December Sunday in 1993, a car pulled into the driveway, and two sober-faced naval officers got out. Lisa and three shipmates had been returning to the academy from a football game. There was a fatal car wreck; three of the shipmates had been killed. One of them was Lisa.

The commander who brought the news could not give us any more information about the crash, not even whose car it had been or who had been driving. The other families had not even been notified yet. All they could tell us was that the accident had occurred in Maryland, not far from the academy, and that, of the vehicle's four occupants, three had died, and the fourth was hospitalized, in serious condition.

Had Lisa been in the driver's seat? She'd recently called home with the news that she'd bought a blue 1985 CJ-7 Jeep, just like the one she'd dreamed about throughout high school. Knowing Lisa, she'd probably already taken it out on back roads at least once or twice, even though she didn't yet have a driver's license. She had been planning to get her license over Christmas break, but if she'd been driving, it had been illegally. I didn't want to have to live with the knowledge that she'd died while breaking the law, taking the lives of others in the process.

As I thought about this prospect, my stomach churned into knots. *Were the other victims people whom we knew?* My mind turned over one name after another: There was Elissa, who'd stayed with us for a long weekend; Becky, the first person Lisa had met at USNA and who had been her roommate off and on for years; Amber, whose exploits over the years had filled Lisa's phone calls; and Enochia, whose crazy sense of humor made me laugh every time we talked. Which dear one's death would we be grieving next, once we learned the details of the crash?

Finally, the news arrived. It had not been the driver's fault— a rotten, rain-soaked tree had fallen on or in front of the car, ripping off the roof. Our Lisa had been thrown from the car. She, along with two other girls, had died at the scene. The driver, Brian, had been Lisa's squad leader, classmate, and good friend, and he'd been rushed to the Shock Trauma Center of the University of Maryland Medical System. He was in serious condition, and he drifted in and out of consciousness for the next few days, unable to remember anything about the accident, unaware that the girls who'd been in his car were dead.

I hadn't known any of the other young women or their families—and I knew that nothing I could do would change their fate. But the driver was a different story. My heart bled for the pain this young man would go through, both physical and mental, if he even survived. Three friends had been killed in his car. When they broke the news to him, would he be tempted to just give up and die, too, even if it wasn't his fault? Would he even be able to believe that it wasn't his fault, with no memories of it all?

I longed to be able to go to his hospital room, hug him tightly, and tell him that he had to get better, that he had to go on living, and that, somehow, for all of us, it would be okay. I felt that this was something I needed to do, something the Lord wanted me to do—but how? Brian was in Maryland. I was in Ohio, and Lisa was being buried there. It would cost a fortune to fly the whole family to Maryland, and there was no way I could leave my other grieving children behind! Still, I knew that if the Lord wanted me to do this, He would make it happen.

Without telling us, some of our friends had decided we needed to go to Maryland, and in no time, they had raised the money for our airplane tickets and set up transportation to and from the airport, while the Navy, at the other end, made housing, food, and transportation arrangements for our stay. By the time we were told about the trip, all we had to do was pack and go. So we did.

Since we were going, there were several things we would be able to take care of in person, but one thing I was adamant about. If Brian was agreeable, the first thing I wanted to do when we arrived was go see him. I didn't say why—how do you explain to naval officers that you feel led by God to go to someone you've never met and tell him to live?—but to my relief, no one ever asked. They just took us to the hospital.

At the door to Brian's room, I hesitated, suddenly unsure. Would he really want to see us? I reminded our escort, "Brian can still change his mind, if he wants to."

"Yes, ma'am, he knows that. But he says he wants to see you."

When we entered his room, Brian was lying on his back, pale and still, wearing a neck brace to prevent any movement of his chipped vertebra. He was staring at the ceiling with an expression of pain and despair on his face that chilled me through and through. I thanked God that He had brought us here, so that I could tell this young man what had been on my heart from the moment I had heard of his plight: "Live!"

Brian slowly turned his head when he realized that there were people in his room. As a well-trained future officer, he spoke first to the officers present. They lightly joked around with him briefly before introducing him to us, one at a time. My oldest son, Mike, shook hands with him, but seemed at a loss for words at the sight of so much pain.

"Hey, man, what's up?"

"Not much...they won't tell me when I can get out of here."

"Does it hurt?"

"Not really. They've got me on pain medicine, though."

Brian thought for a minute, then said, with typical

midshipman understatement, "I tore loose a chunk of scalp on the back of my head, and they had to staple it back on. It doesn't really hurt, though. It just feels a little tight."

After another minute or two of conversation, Mike and my husband, Mark, left the room, and our escorting officers stepped outside to look into Brian's check-out status. Suddenly, Brian and I were alone.

He stared at me for a long time, and tears filled his eyes. Then an anguished cry broke out of him: "I'm so sorry!" I walked over to the bed and put my arms around him. As his shoulders shook with his sobs, I tried desperately not to break down myself. Brian needed me to be strong right now. I had the rest of my life to cry.

"I'm so sorry! If only I had...I can't remember what happened...maybe if we'd left earlier....."

He went on and on, attacking the accident from every angle. The questions and "if-only"s were eating him up, magnified by his not being able to remember anything about that day.

"Shh...ssh," I began to comfort him. "It wasn't your fault! We don't blame you, and Lisa wouldn't either."

I took his hand as we talked, and he clung tightly to it as if to a lifeline. It hurt, but I held on because I knew he needed me. He talked and cried for a long time as I listened and ached for him. When he finally stopped, I got up and put my arms around him again and began to pray for him. I prayed for his healing, for comfort in his grief, for his future in the Navy (unclear at that time, due to his injuries), and for his future relationship with God, the words pouring out of me as though God had opened a pipeline between Himself and Brian, using my heart as a conduit.

As I finished, our escort returned. Brian, holding my hand again, asked them if he was going to be allowed to check out. "Yes, as soon as your parents arrive," the officer replied. "I called their room, but they weren't in. They must be on their way."

When his family piled into his room, they were amazed to see me there and then glad, once they realized who I was. They all began telling me how sorry they were about what happened, and I told them what I had told Brian. I didn't think it was his fault. I didn't blame him. I was glad he had survived and only wanted him to get well and go on with his life. I knew it was important to repeat it all to them. Once Brian went home, he was going to need people around him who could remind him of what I'd said. Who could do that better than his family?

As we left, Brian was sitting up in bed, loudly calling for his clothes and something to eat besides hospital food. He looked like a new man—his color was better, his eyes looked less tortured, and he sounded more alert. I was so glad I'd come! What was it that had turned the tide for him? The hug we'd shared? The prayer? Or was it simply the fact that I had cared enough to come all the way from Ohio to see him? Whatever it was, I'd done what I came to do. Brian was going to live. Now, we could both start to heal.

# $\mathcal{T}$HE COST OF LOVING

## LINDA RONDEAU

*Train up a child in the way he should go: and when he is old,*

*he will not depart from it.*

PROVERBS 22:6

Lisa grabbed Dave's white hankie, conveniently located on the couch. On any other day, she would confront his slovenliness. But today she was grateful for the soiled linen as she wiped away the steady stream of tears from her eyes.

She reached for another cardboard box to finish packing Ashleigh's belongings. She arranged the assortment of musical toys and stuffed animals, unconsciously picking up a white velvet teddy bear, squeezing it tightly against her chest.

It had been a year since Ashleigh had come to live with them. Six years previously, Lisa and Dave felt a call from God to become foster parents. Lisa had always wanted a big family, but after years of waiting, tests, and unanswered prayers, she had to face the possibility she might never conceive.

Lisa knew that God had a different plan. Before she and Dave were married and moved to the city, she had worked for a foster care agency. She knew the urgent need for loving homes in which neglected children could find a nurturing environment. Dave readily supported the idea, prayerfully promising to adopt any of the children in their care should the opportunity arise. After months of specialized training, Lisa and Dave eagerly awaited the first placement.

Baby Michael arrived within a few months. Lisa was thrilled by the joy of holding a tiny one close to her heart. He was their son, no matter how long God allowed him to stay. Lisa found contentment in the hectic, busy days an infant's needs dictated.

A few years later, Cecil arrived. Although he was classified as a special needs child, their love expanded to meet the challenges.

Within a few months, one-year-old Darren entered the home already squeezed by demanding schedules. He was welcomed just the same. Lisa and Dave were told from the beginning that Darren would most likely return to his mother, and they respected that decision, doing all they could to help preserve the relationship between Darren and his birth mother. Knowing from the start that Darren would not be a permanent member of the household did not prepare them for the indescribable sense of loss they felt when the social worker later took him away.

Soon after Darren left, Lisa and Dave received an urgent call from the foster care agency. They had a little boy, two years old, who was in need of a permanent home. The boy, James, had been in foster care since birth, and he'd just been released for adoption. Lisa felt urged to examine the possibility, even though her previously childless home now bulged with toddlers. Michael's adoption was finalized, and it appeared they would also adopt Cecil in the near future. But they also loved James the minute they first saw the affectionate, loving youngster.

Changing diapers, preparing meals, cleaning up, and home schooling the other children, dominated Lisa's days and nights. Yet she still felt a longing for a little girl. She was grateful for the three wonderful boys God had entrusted to her care, but she could not extinguish this unrelenting desire for a daughter.

Within a few weeks of James' final transition into the home, six-month-old Ashleigh came into their care. Lisa and Dave fell in love with her gurgles and wide-eyed grins the minute she arrived. They relished in her spunk, curiosity, and good nature as she crawled behind her new big brothers, following them from room to room, and even getting into the act when Daddy played roughhouse with the boys. Her presence seemed as natural as the sunrise. Lisa never considered the two family additions within the month a burden. She refused to even think of Ashleigh's possible return to her birth mother. Echoes of the pain she felt when Darren had been removed from their home were stifled by the pleasure she found in Ashleigh's antics.

Lisa knew the cost of being a foster parent was lifelong heart pangs when a child returned to an uncertain future. But it was different when it came to her only little girl. She pressed the teddy bear closer to her body. Seeking solace and comfort she said a prayer in her heart. She released the plush toy, then wiped her eyes again, and sealed the box.

That evening, Lisa sat solemnly during the Ladies Prayer Circle. Her heart felt as if a thousand-pound weight was crushing it. She thought it best not to mention Ashleigh's leaving. Her grief was so pervasive she feared that speaking of it aloud would unleash a torrent of emotions that would leave her unable to care for the other children in her charge. The leader passed around a bowl of Bible verses. Each participant was instructed to take one out to read to the group.

Lisa was stunned when she opened the piece of paper to read, "He tends his flock like a shepherd: He gathers the lambs in his arms and carries them close to his heart" (Isaiah 40:11). She gasped at God's perfect timing, no longer able to restrain the flow of tears. Finally sharing her need, she was comforted by her friends' prayers on behalf of Ashleigh, for her ultimate salvation and the salvation of her birth parents. Lisa knew God would fill the hole in her life with other children, but that Ashleigh's imprint would always remain. God had allowed this precious jewel into their lives for a purpose yet unknown.

As the prayers came to a close, Lisa felt a release from the tightness that had compressed her heart, finding solace in the knowledge that The Good Shepherd had a plan for Ashleigh, even though that plan would be fulfilled apart from her watchful eye.

# $\mathscr{I}$ LOVE YOU, CAITLIN

## STEPHANIE JACOBS

*We know how much God loves us, and we have put our trust in him.*

*God is love, and all who live in love live in God, and God lives in them.*

1 J O H N 4 : 1 6 NLT

I stood in the brightly lit hospital lobby holding my baby daughter, Caitlin. Born prematurely, she had spent six tortuous weeks in intensive care and was at last being released to go home. I tried to concentrate on the barrage of instructions a nurse was giving me for her care. "You'll do fine," she finally finished, patting me on the shoulder. I wished I could be so confident. I glanced at my two-year-old son, Patrick, crawling between chair legs nearby. *I've done okay with one child,* I tried to reassure myself. *I can handle another one.* But Patrick had always been a healthy baby. Caitlin had already been on the brink of death. At home there would be no machine to sound an alarm if there were an emergency, no nurse standing by to help.

My hands shook as I tried to buckle Caitlin into her infant seat in our van. "Let me," my husband, Carl, intervened. He looked at me. "Hey, this is a happy day, remember," he said, brushing away a tear that was sliding down my cheek.

At home I settled into the wide oak rocker with her in the nursery Carl and I had painted yellow and decorated with mobiles. *I'm on my own now,* I thought. I took off Caitlin's bonnet and unbuttoned her pink sweater. I had wanted so much to give Patrick a sibling, but as I traced my finger along the scars on Caitlin's chest and stroked her shaved head, I wondered how I would handle the added responsibility of a child who already had so many health problems.

I wrapped her in a warm blanket and held her against my shoulder. "Hello there, Caitlin," I cooed, rocking slowly.

Patrick clambered up on my lap and squinted at his little sister. "What color are her eyes, Mama?" he asked.

With a start I realized I couldn't say for sure. Caitlin had been sedated or asleep most of the time since her birth. I had never really gotten a good look at her eyes. I held her in front of me, but she turned away. "Look at Mama, Caitlin," I cajoled, peering at her pale face. She kept her eyes tightly closed. "We'll know in time," I assured Patrick. Yet I felt a twinge of frustration that after all the time I had waited to hold my daughter, I would have to wait even longer to know one of the most fundamental things about her.

It was in December that the first labor pains brought me to my knees while I was tending our weather-battered rose garden. At the hospital, doctors gave me medication to halt the contractions and ordered complete bed rest until my April due date.

I had spent the long days on the couch staring out the picture windows, monitoring the time between contractions, and thinking of the son who had been stillborn the previous year after similar complications. I breathed a sigh of relief each time I watched the final few pink streaks of sunset fade into the indigo twilight. Another day closer to a full-term, healthy baby.

It was a drizzly March morning when the contractions couldn't be held off any longer. In the delivery room I reached for my husband's hand as the doctor rushed Caitlin away. "Only a few weeks early," a nurse said to me. "She'll be okay." But she wasn't. Caitlin was flown 40 miles to a neonatal intensive care unit in Houston, where doctors gently prepared me for the worst. Day after day I hoped for a miracle. Seeing her limbs flail as she struggled to get free of the tangle of needles and tubes keeping her alive, I had to look away. *God, please help,* I prayed.

Then, suddenly, Caitlin took a turn for the better. Before I knew it, the doctors were bidding good-bye to the child they had dubbed a "miracle girl." Yet, gazing at her fragile body in the comforting dimness of our own nursery, I felt the same anxiety I had felt while she was in my womb—she was once again in my charge. Patrick scrambled off to play and I placed Caitlin in her crib. "Mama's going to look after you," I murmured, but I shivered at the thought of what might lie in store.

Every day I carefully spoon-fed Caitlin, only to watch her spit up time after time. Terrified that her breathing would stop during the night, I moved her crib into our bedroom and slept with one hand on her bony shoulder. Often, I woke up and placed my palm against her chest, checking for her heartbeat. *Why has she had to go through so much?* I thought.

"Caitlin, I love you," I said over and over, but she always kept her face turned away, her eyes squeezed shut. Each time she flinched when I touched her, it felt like rejection. Gazing at her one night, I was filled with a loneliness I had never known before.

The more I thought about it, the more my hurt swelled. I had been let down in life many times. Like with Dad. After suspending my education to help care for him when he got sick, I had watched him die at age 47. And Dean. My high school friend had been killed in a car accident after rushing to help with a family crisis. I stood at Caitlin's crib long into the night, thinking about the sore spots in my memory, the wounds that had never really healed.

During the following days I felt more and more helpless about Caitlin's unresponsiveness.

"Patience," Carl reminded me. "She's still not used to the outside world." But I took her to the pediatrician. The doctor examined her and assured me she was aware of her surroundings and that her physical condition was, in fact, improving.

"Caitlin is ignoring you," she said. "It's a phenomenon I've seen in infants who have received long-term care in trauma units. I think they may be refusing to look their caretakers in the face because they associate them with pain."

Could that possibly be true? I would have done anything to protect her from harm, to erase all the hurt she had already experienced. Yet she linked me with suffering!

That night I settled in the rocker with my sleeping baby. Never before had she seemed so far away from me, not even when she was being kept alive by machines and I wasn't allowed to touch her. I looked at her, cradled against my arm, her head turned away from me as usual. I bent over and softly kissed her. *I would never want to hurt her,* I thought sadly, I only want to comfort her. I caressed her cheek gently with my finger.

*Why so much pain, God?* With that question, Caitlin's behavior reminded me of someone—me. Hadn't I been turning away from God, blaming him for the hurtful things that had happened in my life just as my baby daughter was associating her own pain with me? God hated the sadness I had suffered just as much as I hated all Caitlin had gone through. Perhaps my resentment had wounded God just as deeply as my daughter's avoidance was hurting me.

New thoughts surfaced. How Caitlin had survived despite all the odds. How I would never have met Carl had I not gone home to care for Dad when he fell ill. I saw each sorrow from a new perspective, saw how I had been guided and helped through the hard times, how—though I had thought I was alone—and yet, God had watched over me just as devotedly as I was watching over Caitlin.

*I'm sorry, Father,* I whispered. *I know now I can turn to you.* I looked down at Caitlin.

*Please help me get through to her.*

The next day I rolled Caitlin's crib to the nursery. I fastened pictures of family and friends to the crib's rails, surrounding her with loving faces whose gazes she could not avoid. I took her to the garden with me when I watered and fertilized the sickly roses. But she still turned away and scrunched her eyes tight when I touched her.

Caring for her still took all my energy, but I no longer felt so anxious. When I got frustrated, even with simple things like trying to change her diaper or give her a bath, I reached out to

God for help. Caitlin began keeping down her food. Her breathing became stronger. Each night I smoothed lotion onto her scars. "These will fade," I promised her. *So will the emotional ones,* I told myself.

Caitlin continued to grow healthier, but she still would not face me. "Let me see those pretty eyes of yours," I wheedled. Every time she turned away, I whispered, "Caitlin, I love you! Even if you never look at me, I love you."

One warm morning I stood in the garden, surrounded by rosebushes laden with colorful blooms. Caitlin dawdled on a blanket at my feet. I picked a red rose and, kneeling, brushed the velvety petals lightly across Caitlin's own rosy cheek. "I love you, Caitlin!" I said for the umpteenth time that day.

And then—finally—she looked at me. I caught my breath and gazed into her big eyes. They were green with gold flecks, the color of a sunlit forest. They were the most beautiful sight on earth. In that one look I saw God's love and I felt the joy He must feel every time one of his children acknowledges that love. I had chosen to love my daughter God's way, and in turn, He had given me an even greater glimpse of the love that He had for me—and for us all.

# My LITTLE MAN

## LENA HUNT MABRA

*Children are a gift from the LORD; they are a reward from him.*

PSALM 127:3 NLT

*A mother's letter to her thirteen-year-old son speaks of the message that God had sent her.*

My Little Man,

No longer a boy but not yet a man. I'm sorry if you don't like your nickname, but this is how I see you. Thirteen years old, and I feel as if I'd just given birth to you a few days ago. If only I could hold on and keep you under my constant care like I did when you were younger. But you are growing so fast, and I must let you do the things you love. I must slowly let you go.

"Wear your helmet," I firmly stated as you prepared to leave for a day of skating with your friends.

"I've never worn it before," you told me, rolling your eyes and exhaling loudly.

"I know and that's my fault. With the tricks you are doing, you either wear it or you just don't go." I gave you the ultimatum, trying to protect you even as you left to catch your ride. As I watched the truck pull away, I felt my heart leaving with you.

I've been so consumed with our job losses and the bills. I know you understand even though you've been going on your merry way leaving me to deal with my worries. You quit asking me to watch you skateboard, knowing that I have more important things to do.

You've patiently waited while Dad and I discussed over and over what we will do about our situation. You even added your boyish suggestion: "Just go tell your old boss what you think!" Oh, if only it were that easy, Son.

As usual, the minute you walked in the door I began to scold you about the unfinished lawn and your war-zone bedroom. "How many times have I told you to clean up that...."

"Mom! Dad! I got hit on the head with a metal bar today," you interrupted my complaining. That was when I noticed the dark crusted blood trail which started at the crown of your head and ended at the forehead. My heart sank. Words cannot possibly describe how a mother feels when her children are hurt.

"Why didn't you wear your helmet?" I was furious! You told me you did wear it when you were skating, but you were hit while walking with your friends on the sidewalk. Just for fun, your friend kicked up an iron bar and threw it up in the air.

The bar came down, and you collapsed to the ground.

God, don't let me die! Don't let me die! was your prayer. The blood oozed down your face. Someone covered your head with a cap, but the dark, black-red blood soaked it in a matter of minutes. You were so scared, but you tried to remain calm.

No one called me. Your dad and I didn't know what had happened until you were home. I thank God that you knew to pray. I thank God that you weren't severely hurt and that miraculously, the metal was diverted a few inches away from your face and eyes. Thank God you weren't looking up and that the bar hadn't hit any harder. A few slight changes and, my son, our lives could have been completely changed.

Oh, but my life has changed. I'm sorry that I've been so wrapped up in worries and chores. Maybe I can't keep you home with me like when you were younger. Maybe I can't make you wear a helmet while walking on the sidewalk with your friends. But I can forgive the unfinished lawn. I can even overlook the bedroom war zone, as long as there is a walking path.

I can make time to watch you do your tricks without focusing on the black marks that you leave on the driveway. The chores and the worries will always be here but you, "My Little Man," are only with me for a short while. Thank you for changing my life.

Love,
Mom

# $\mathcal{G}$IVEN TO GOD

## LINDA HENSON

*By wisdom a house is built, and through understanding it is established.*

PROVERBS 24:3 NIV

Is it possible for a newborn daughter to save the life of her mother? That's what happened in my case. All through the pregnancy Jim and I had problems. Everything started out so beautifully. Jim had a promising career as a minister, and I had always dreamed of becoming a pastor's wife. I thought we had the perfect marriage. After all, ministers taught others about faithfulness and purity. We were both young, attractive, and totally in love; people often commented that we were the perfect couple.

Everything was wonderful until Jim began to spend a lot of time with a new group of friends. It wasn't long afterward that it became common for Jim to be out all night—rarely accounting for his evenings. Jim didn't even try to hide his activities. He actually had convinced himself that it was the "cool" thing to

---

"FAMILY FACES ARE LIKE MAGIC MIRRORS. LOOKING AT PEOPLE WHO BELONG TO US, WE SEE THE PAST, PRESENT, AND FUTURE. WE MAKE DISCOVERIES ABOUT OURSELVES."

*Gail Lumet Buckley*

do. After all, his other close friends were doing it.

Then came the yearly "guy" thing. When he left for the annual meeting, I would feel sick inside. I could see his whole attitude deteriorate. Family life seemed less and less important to him. We began to argue a lot. Fear had overtaken me; fear of losing my home and our life together. I couldn't believe we had sunk to such depths. We believed the Bible, but it played less and less of a part in our lives. It had become just a source book, something Jim used as the basis for his weekly homily.

Our relationship was suffering. I could see I was losing my husband and I didn't handle any of it in a righteous way. I accused, criticized, cried, and totally aggravated the situation. We were both on a downhill spiral.

I began to toy with thoughts of ending the pain. Each time I opened the medicine cabinet I stared at the bottles of different types of pills and wondered which ones could be lethal in large doses.

In the midst of all the pain I found out I was pregnant. Through the months of my pregnancy, my swollen body didn't make me feel any better. My days seemed to grow darker and darker.

One morning the pains began, and only two hours later I was holding a bright shining light. In the midst of my darkness God had sent an angel to brighten my days. In my desperation I clung to that sweet baby girl—but it didn't seem to be enough. One day, at a weak moment, I put the baby in her crib and went to the closet where we kept a handgun high on the shelf. I tiptoed, stretched, and finally felt the cold, dark steel in my hand. I pulled it down and held it in both hands, thinking of the decision before me.

I heard a small cry from the crib, and I looked down into the face of my angel. I began to imagine what her life would be like growing up knowing that her mother had done such a thing. Somewhere deep inside I heard a voice saying, *I didn't create you for this.* I fell to my knees and began to cry. I knew that God cared about my situation and had spoken to me. Sobs poured from the very depths of my heart. I felt I was at the bottom of a deep well, but as I looked up, I could see the light. Repentance poured from my soul to the ears of God. I lifted my baby from her bed and held her tightly.

It seemed I held on to her for days. One day at a time, I sought God's help to restore my life and mental attitude. I realized that I had to deal with my own attitudes and only God could change my husband. Little by little I felt inner healing taking place and to my surprise, the more I released my husband's problems to God, the more I saw change take place in him. We were becoming a close-knit family again.

Just as we were experiencing the hand of God on our lives, a small church on the other side of the state requested that we come. I knew it was divine leading. We were finally ready to be the spiritual leaders we had been "called" to be. My daughter was still a source of inspiration to me, but I knew that perhaps I clung to her more than I should.

When she was five years old she caught a cold that didn't seem to go away. On Christmas Eve she was terribly ill. Finally, I couldn't stand it any longer and insisted we rush her to the emergency room. She had a high fever and as I held her in the car, I was terrified that we would lose her. All the way to the hospital, I prayed. I wept and clung tightly to the small form in the blanket. As we pulled into the hospital, I whispered, *God, she's Yours. I give her to You. Please take care of her.*

The doctors swept her from my arms. Nurses ushered us into the waiting room. Waiting rooms seem to scream with pain—wives wondering if their husbands will survive heart attacks, children wondering if their mothers will return home; pain is everywhere.

It seemed like an eternity before anyone returned to speak to us. A nurse came to relate the doctor's message: "It's possible that she has spinal meningitis." The words sent a chill through me. I called my mother, who knows how to pray. Others from our church were praying too. All night we prayed, sometimes in the chapel, sometimes at her bedside.

In the wee hours of the morning the nurse came into our room and told us that she was out of danger; she only had pneumonia—and they could treat pneumonia. At that moment, I began to rejoice and thank God.

Through the years my daughter and I have shared a very special bond. What a delight she has been to me.

Now grown, my daughter travels abroad in diplomatic service and I know that she is in situations of potential danger much of the time. But long ago, and with great trust, I placed her in the hands of an ever faithful God. She belongs to Him, though I believe with all of my heart she was put into my life as a special gift from the Father.

# $\mathscr{T}$HE MIRROR

## LINDA HENSON

*If we are living in the light of God's presence, just as Christ does, then we*
*have wonderful fellowship and joy with each other.*

1 JOHN 1:7 TLB

I trembled a bit as I slowly slipped my finger under the seal of the envelope. Both of my daughters are strong, productive young women who reluctantly agreed to my proposal. I had just finished my first year of graduate studies in counseling. The first year is the hardest; each student is required to receive ten hours of personal counseling. I didn't think I had anything that needed "fixing;" on the outside we were a happy, balanced family. I had discovered that you can't help others if you can't look at yourself. As the layers ripped off through those sessions, I began to feel exposed. Maybe I wasn't as "OK" as I had thought.

I did the scariest thing I could imagine. I called each of my daughters and asked them to write me a letter telling me what they felt about my parenting. I asked them for a "no-holds-barred" response. The weeks of waiting for their replies were horrendous for me. My mind went through every experience I could remember, wondering if the girls would say I was unfair, or too hard on them. It was an open invitation for them to let me have it. Painful as it might be, I truly wanted to know. I wondered, *Could I learn from the past?*

I was the disciplinarian in our family. My husband is an easy-going phlegmatic who likes to be the good guy. I was raised with rules and regulations and had learned that there was a price to pay when rules were broken. My siblings and I all seemed to be responsible adults, so I assumed that the parenting model I had experienced was the best one to follow.

My counseling sessions had proven to be heart-wrenching. It was necessary to look at the effect of our parents' input into our lives. I've always struggled with this part of counseling; I need to take responsibility for the choices I've made and refuse to blame my parents. It was important to realize that our past shapes the way we handle life, so I was forced to hold up a mirror to my life and willingly see the negative aspects of the model my parents set before me.

My mother was very controlling; everyone knew she spoke for the family. My dad went along with whatever she wanted just to survive. I began to let the memories come back. I felt the fear of my mother's wrath. Did I receive beatings? No, but the fear was there. Even the look of disapproval, disappointment, or the tone of voice from a parent can go deep into a child's heart, and I realized my heart had been pierced.

One Saturday while I was a teen, a group of teenagers from our local church planned a day at the State Park. It was too cool to swim so we knew we'd have to look for other activities such as hiking or boating. My mother had never learned to swim, and she was determined that we wouldn't go near the water if she wasn't around. I happened to mention that I needed money to help pay for the rental of a rowboat.

"You are not to go out in a boat!" was her order.

"But, Mom, that's what everybody will do."

"You heard me."

I was right. Everyone in the group rented boats and spent the day on the water. I sat alone on the beach all afternoon. Why didn't I just go ahead and go with the rest of the group? Somehow, the fear of Mom finding out was so strong that a miserable afternoon seemed easier to take. There was a mental control that followed me through much of my life. I hadn't realized it until the counselor held up the "mirror."

During my engagement to my husband we would return home after a date and sit in the driveway for a few minutes before going inside with the family. Of course, we weren't going to go "too far" with my parents right inside; but invariably, my mother would begin to flash the porch light on and off, signaling that we were to come in immediately. Not all of the fear was bad. It kept me from making mistakes that could have had negative impacts on my life. There is a measure of parental fear that is healthy. However, the line is very easy to cross and after experiencing the counseling, I feared that I could have easily stepped over it with my own children without realizing it. Only they could decide, and I was about to read their assessments.

Had I imparted that same controlling fear to my daughters? Did they see me as I saw my mother? Children see our imperfections and learn to live with them. Did my daughters have to find mechanisms to deal with the kind of parent I had been? All of these questions ran through my mind as I tore away the envelope that held my older daughter's response.

Tears flowed down my cheeks as kindness flowed through her words. I had asked for harsh truth and yet I received beautiful compliments. Most of the letter reminisced the good moments we had enjoyed. At the end, though, was this thought:

*Mom, I wish you had talked to me more.*

I was startled. We had talked. But I realized her desire. I was never open to sharing my thoughts, pain, or longings with her. I understood that she didn't know who I really was. She knew me as one who fed, clothed, and provided emotional support, but in my desire to be the picture of a good mother, I had withheld the real me.

The second letter stared at me. Our older daughter had always been an easy-to-please child who gave little or no resistance to our directions, but the second? She was another story. It seemed she always pushed the line. She had an outlook on life that said, "I think I can fly!" Now, I was about to read her opinions on my parenting skills. I braced myself. We had butted heads repeatedly through her teen years. But, to my amazement, her letter began as the first, with sharing the things she appreciated. Tears would not describe my response. Opened floodgates might be a better reflection of the scene.

When I read the second part of her letter, I nearly dropped the page. I decided the girls had collaborated, for I read nearly the same phrase:

*Mom, I wish you had shared who you are with me.*

I ran to the phone and called each one of them asking if they had talked and agreed upon their responses; but each assured me they had not spoken about what went into their letters. Actually, they had been as nervous about writing them as I had been about reading them.

Following my telephone conversations with the girls, I had

to go to God. I had hidden behind walls that now were revealed. Could I trust that He would heal the hurts and ease the pain as I bared my inner self?

In the days since, I've made a conscious effort to take special times with each of my daughters to sit and talk with them openly. I've shared times of my life that were full of pain. I've shared embarrassing moments. I hadn't realized that withholding some of the unlovely things of my life had presented a level of perfection to them that they felt they could never attain. It is a relief to find that sharing my imperfections has drawn us closer together. With a lot of hard work and dedication, the love of two amazing daughters, and the tender grace of a merciful God, we have all been set free to love each other completely—without reservation.

# THE IDEAL FAMILY THAT WASN'T

## SHARON HINCK

*Let us not become weary in doing good, for at the proper time*

*we will reap a harvest if we do not give up.*

GALATIANS 6:9 NIV

My son Joel is vacuuming his room. I listen from the family room and notice that my eyes are beginning to sting. I tell myself I'm just moved to tears of joy because he's vacuuming, and blink back my true feelings. After he finishes cleaning, he'll take the last box of books and clothes out to his car. Joel is heading back to college for his sophomore year.

I thought I was done with the tears. After all, a year ago I helped him load the van and drive to the campus. I released him with one last hug, watching him, small and thin against the large dorm building as he walked away. The aching pull in my chest was familiar. It was just like the time his tiny face had pressed against the school bus window, waving good-bye on his first day of kindergarten. I wanted to stop the bus and cry, "Wait! It's too soon! He isn't ready!" But he was more than ready...thirteen years ago on that school bus, one year ago in front of his new dorm room, and today as he juggles a tall CD rack up the stairs and out to the car.

Summer didn't give us the time to catch up that I had hoped. The whole family struggled with the awkwardness of having a new, "grown-up" Joel in the house.

Near the end of summer we celebrated with Joel when he and Jennelle got engaged. She is everything we dreamed of in a daughter-in-law, and I find myself smiling when I watch them together. They glow. But their happiness means that this fall, "cleaning out the room" is happening for the last time. Next summer they will start their own home. He will never be back. Not in the same way.

My emotions are a hard, taut lump. It reminds me of a project my youngest daughter Jenny created. She formed a ball by wrapping rubber bands around each other layer by layer. An ultrasound of my heart would match it exactly.

In my mind, I begin to carefully pull away the various colored rubber bands to sort out my feelings, hoping I won't snap in the process.

Of course I feel joy. That is an easy band to separate from the lump. I'm so proud of the young man Joel has become, and happy for the Christian college that has continued to shape and form him. But there is also a very tight, thin band of anxiety. He's still so young, and there are many challenges ahead for him and Jennelle. There is relief somewhere in the bundle of feelings as well. He has weathered the struggles of adolescence and his first year of independence, and he stood firm. But there is a twisted strand of loneliness. I thought that with three younger children still at home, I'd be too busy to feel this—but I just plain miss him.

As I pry deeper into my thoughts and feelings, I come to the core. As Joel gets ready to leave home, there is a tight ball of regret in the center of my emotions.

When Ted and I got married, I dreamed of what our family life would be like. My dream family was heavily influenced by Louisa May Alcott's book, *The Five Little Peppers,* and the movie "The Sound of Music." In my imagination we would sit by a fireplace reading Bible stories to children gathered at our feet. We would sing together and play instruments like a modern Von Trapp family. We would talk about everything together, pray with each other often, and never be sucked into the materialism and hyperactivity of our culture.

Family life didn't end up looking like I had imagined all those years ago.

Yes, there were family devotions. But often one of the

children begged us to speed things along. In the early years there were story times and cozy talks at bedtime. But those grew shorter and more hurried as time went by.

There were times we made music together—with our voices or with various instruments. But it was an occasional thing, not a routine of life as I had once dreamed.

What went wrong?

Like an old fashioned filmstrip, static images stream past my eyes in the glare of a bare, hot light bulb. Instead of the cozy, placid family by the hearth, I see a night at the emergency room and remember the panic as Joel struggled for breath against the asthma that squeezed him.

There weren't the family vacations I had once envisioned. Instead there were long stretches of unemployment, struggle, and effort to keep food on the table. But there was also the mission trip to Hong Kong. I see the image of Paolo, a wonderful man from Samoa, teaching Joel how to climb a palm tree using just his hands and feet. Instead of quiet bedtimes, I see many evenings with people at our home—music and laughter in the living room, toddlers playing under the table.

The next image in my mental filmstrip snags and the edges begin to melt. I see the visits to friends in the hospital, and the funerals that cut at our hearts and steal away our music for a time.

In recent years, with a home full of older children, my ideal family had been brushed aside by the revolving door of activities. Just showing up for each other's events filled many evenings. Josh and Jenny in a musical at church, Katie's band concert, Joel's school play. Family reunions, birthday parties, a cousin's wedding, a nephew's graduation, piano recitals. Often four events collided on the same tiny square of the calendar, and our tension grew, words becoming tight and irritated.

The filmstrip slows for a moment. That was the year we home schooled. The pace calmed. We sat together in the living room and read out loud. We walked slowly around the pond and noticed each different wildflower.

The images pick up speed again and flash past my memory. There is so much rushing, so many arguments about chores and curfews. Laughing around the table, whining about lentils for supper, kicking a sister under the table, spilt milk....

And today I'm sitting out in the family room, listening to Joel vacuuming his room.

The hard tight ball of regret softens and rolls gently away.

We gave Joel a home. A crazy, inconsistent, interesting home. It wasn't the ideal family I had pictured. But it was textured and rich with experiences. God's grace was able to cast light on the filmstrip of our life—and bring a glow into the imperfections.

Yes, there is plenty I want to improve on with the other

three. There is still too much snipping at each other. Too much television. Too much hyperactivity that leaves us feeling like five roommates sharing a home instead of a cohesive family unit. But there are too few minutes in the day to fully savor the family life we have—I can't spare any more minutes regretting the family life we don't have. Besides, the dream of family life is God's dream, not just mine. He is working out a plan for my children, and I'm just a little part of that picture.

The noise of the vacuum stops, and the house is heavily silent. Joel is standing behind me. "Well, g'bye," he says awkwardly. And, in an act even more rare than his pushing the vacuum cleaner, he opens his arms for a hug. As I squeeze him tightly and then let him go, I think about the ideal family he will soon work to build. I know it will end up looking very different than what he imagines today. But God's blessings will infuse each day and bring constant surprises. His not-quite-ideal family will be wonderful.

# 𝒜 NEW BEGINNING

## PAT SELLERS

*Weeping may remain for a night, but joy comes in the morning.*

PSALM 30:5 NIV

The sky was a blinding blue that October afternoon, the kind of crisp Autumn day our boys loved. I was imagining Brent, 5, and Blake, 3, tearing across our yard and with a whoop, leaping into the huge pile of leaves their big brother, Scott, 13, had raked.

Except that was never going to happen again. Blake was dead, victim of a strain of bacterial meningitis so vicious it snuffed out his life in the space of a few hours. Instead of watching him climb the oak tree out front, hearing him laugh with delight when he made it higher than before, we were laying him to rest.

A sob escaped me, and my husband, Jeff, squeezed my hand tighter as we stood beside our son's grave. The service had ended, punctuated by the thuds of car doors as mourners left the cemetery. But we couldn't bring ourselves to leave Blake. Not yet.

"HAPPINESS LIES IN WAIT; IT COMES UPON US SUDDENLY, LIKE A MIDNIGHT THIEF AT A TURN UP IN THE STREET, OR IN THE MIDST OF A DREAM, BECAUSE A RAY OF LIGHT, A STRAIN OF MUSIC, A FACE, OR A GESTURE HAS OVERCOME THE DESPAIR OF LIVING."

*Hector Biancotti*

Finally our pastor slid an arm around each of us and led us away from the small mound of newly turned dirt. "Pat, Jeff," he said, "saying good-by to your son was probably the hardest thing you've ever done. But I have to warn you, the months ahead will be even tougher."

I didn't see how anything could be worse than losing Blake.

"A loss like this puts a terrible strain on a marriage," he continued. "Couples end up divorced. I'm not saying that's going to happen to you, but don't be afraid to ask for help."

*We won't need help,* I thought. Nothing could destroy our marriage.

"You don't have to worry about us," Jeff said firmly. "Pat and I will get through this the way we get through everything—together."

For days afterward I was never far from Jeff, nor he from me. We tried to be strong in front of the boys. It was best for them if things settled down and returned to normal.

Privately I wondered if they ever would. Even the simple act of waking up wasn't the same. Jeff and I used to savor the early morning—before work, chores and the kids came rushing at us. We'd talk a while, holding each other. Then I'd listen as Jeff said a prayer. It made us feel centered to start the day with a quiet moment together. But now we couldn't find the peace, no matter how we clung to each other. At night we'd lie side by

side, sleepless, then slip into a fitful doze only to be startled
awake by the alarm clock.

One morning a week after the funeral Jeff asked, "You
awake, Babe?"

"I couldn't sleep."

"Neither could I," he said. "I've been thinking....I'm going
back to work today."

"You can't!" I cried. "It's too soon."

"I have to," Jeff said. "They need me at the store." He
managed his family's hardware business, and I knew he couldn't
be away from it for long. But what would I do all day on my own?

"Don't leave me," I pleaded, clutching his arm.

He eased out of my grip, out of bed, and started getting
ready. Before he left he kissed me on the forehead and told me
reassuringly, "You'll be okay, Babe. Call me."

I wasn't okay. Not even close. After I got Scott and Brent
off to school, I crept back to bed, exhausted from the effort of
trying to be cheerful for them. Around lunchtime, still in my
nightgown, I dragged myself into the kitchen. Mechanically, I
lined up bread, peanut butter and grape jelly on the counter and
began assembling a sandwich. I trimmed the crust off the
bread. *Just the way Blake likes it,* I thought.

With a jolt, I realized what I was doing. I bolted from the
kitchen and flung myself on Blake's bed, stifling my sobs in

his pillow. "My sweet baby," I whispered. Late in the afternoon I heard the rumble of a school bus. I can't let the boys see me like this. I forced myself to get up and get dressed.

When Jeff came in that evening, he asked with a hopeful smile, "How'd it go today?"

"It was awful," I replied. "I barely made it out of bed."

"Oh, Babe," he said, pulling me close. "It'll get better."

As the weeks passed, it did seem to get easier—for Jeff. He had his work. But for me, the ache of loss only deepened. Laundry, cooking and cleaning became mere drudgery, no longer games to dawdle over with my little helper, Blake, at my heels. Without him chattering away, an oppressive silence pervaded the house. At first I left the TV on, but the songs on Sesame Street reminded me how Blake loved Big Bird. I'd catch myself peering out the window, waiting for Scott and Brent to get home from school and rescue me from my loneliness.

By the time Jeff got home I was desperate for his company. As soon as we were alone, I dug in. One evening he got in bed and settled back with a magazine. He hadn't turned a page before I announced, "We need to talk."

A pained expression crept over his face. He knew what was coming. "I'll be glad to listen," he said. "Just please don't ask me to talk about Blake. I can't anymore."

"I really have to go over what happened that last day," I insisted. For the next half hour I recounted every agonizing detail. I almost forgot Jeff was there, until he touched my arm. "Be right back," he said and disappeared into the bathroom. When he didn't emerge I glared at the closed door. Why didn't he want to talk about Blake? They had been so close, so alike. Didn't Jeff miss him the way I did, so much that it physically hurt?

Months slipped by, and we stumbled on through the uncharted territory of grief. Near dawn one morning I lay in bed listening to Jeff's even breathing, getting angrier and angrier. Our little boy was dead, and he was sleeping as if nothing were wrong! I don't know what got into me, but I gave him a swift poke in the ribs.

"What?" he mumbled sleepily.

"You were snoring."

"Sorry." He sat up, awake. "Babe," he said, taking my hand, "don't you think it's time we went back to our morning prayer?"

"I can't pray to a God who didn't save my child," I said, pulling away, the bitterness in my own voice frightening me.

"Then I'll pray for you," he said softly.

"I don't need your prayers!" They can't comfort me, and neither can you, I added silently.

It became harder for us to live in our home without Blake.

Brent refused to sleep in the bedroom they had shared. We all avoided that room, still filled with Blake's clothes, toys and lingering little-boy smell. But no matter where we went in the house, something called forth the memory of the sunny-faced toddler whose giggles still echoed in our minds.

One evening as Jeff helped me clear the table, he offered a solution. "I think we should move," he said. "Maybe it'll give us a new start. I want us to be a family again."

I nodded warily. I wanted that too, but I was beginning to wonder if the warning our pastor had given us was coming true.

"Most of all," Jeff added, his gaze resting on me tenderly, "I want my girl back."

"That girl is gone forever," I snapped, not thinking. "Just like Blake." Immediately I felt bad, but it was too late to take it back.

We looked for a house for months, with no luck. Finally, we decided to build our own. After long days at the store, Jeff grabbed quick suppers with us, then rushed out to work on the house, leaving me alone with the boys. The tension between us escalated. We had rarely exchanged a harsh word in all our years of marriage. Now we bickered constantly. He was determined to stay within budget, and I didn't see the point of building a home if we had to cut corners. We stopped smiling at each other, stopped touching. That patient "I'm praying for you" expression on Jeff's face infuriated me. The qualities that had once drawn me to him—his quiet strength, his steadiness—left me cold.

One day after a nasty skirmish, I caught Jeff muttering, "That woman will send us to the poorhouse!"

I felt a stab of hurt and a sudden, dreadful revelation: Somehow I had gone from being his "Babe" to "that woman."

"I'm sick of this!" I cried, powerless to stem the rush of angry words from my lips. "I'm sick of pretending everything's okay between us. Maybe we should call it quits!"

The air vibrated with a silence more terrible than that which filled the house after Blake died.

Then Jeff took me by the shoulders and held me, more with his solemn gaze than with his touch. "Pat," he said, his voice breaking, "as much as Blake loved our family, how do you think he would feel if his death split us up?"

Blake. Our family. Love. Like arrows hitting their mark, the words pierced the armor of anger I had isolated myself in, not just from my husband but from God. With something like relief, I sank into Jeff's arms. Together we wept for our son, and for what our grief had done to our marriage.

"Going on without Blake is hard enough," Jeff whispered, gently tracing the tracks of my tears with his thumb. "I can't make it without you."

"I can't make it without you either," I said. I had been so

wrapped up in my pain that I hadn't seen Jeff had been hurting too, in his own quiet way. I reached up and pressed his hand to my cheek. "I need you."

It was a beginning. We made time for each other again, every day, not necessarily for long talks but simply to be together. I saw a counselor who guided me in coping with my grief. Jeff brought me in to work part-time at the store. Each small change was a step toward him, toward love and healing.

As much work as we put into our new house, we put more into building a new life together. It wouldn't be the same without Blake. It couldn't. But even though God's way for us wasn't at first what I had wanted it to be, it was still good. I finally knew this was true when early one spring morning I heard Jeff say, "Thank You, God, for all you've given us. Our children, our health…" I found myself holding him closer and adding, "…and our love for each other, and for You."

# TIMMY'S RING

## NANCY C. ANDERSON

*You have formed my inward parts; you have covered me in my mother's*

*womb. I will praise You, for I am fearfully and wonderfully made.*

PSALM 139:13-14 NKJV

My new neighbor touched my hand and said, "What a lovely ring; it looks like an antique. It's so unusual—where did you get it?"

I replied slowly, carefully choosing my words. "I had it custom made."

She said, "I have a friend who's a jeweler. Would you mind if I copied it?"

I said, "First, let me tell you the story behind the design."

It was just after New Year's Day in 1990 when I found out I was pregnant with our second child. My husband, Ron, was thrilled, but I was apprehensive. Our five-year-old, Nick, had several learning disabilities, and he was quite a "handful." I told Ron, "I'm afraid I won't have enough energy to care for

Nick and a newborn baby."

I went for all the required checkups, and the doctor assured me that everything was fine. However, since I would be thirty-five when the baby was born, and that meant I had a higher chance of a baby with birth defects, the doctor wanted to do an ultrasound.

I tried to find a comfortable position on the hard examination table as the nurse's aide squirted the cold sonogram gel on my expanding belly. One technician slid the scope over my stomach as the other one watched the monitor. I looked at the woman who was watching my baby on the screen. Her face didn't have much expression. And then, suddenly, it did.

Her eyes widened and her hands flew involuntarily to her mouth as she made a sad squeaking sound. "What's wrong?" I cried. I sat up and repeated my question. She tried to compose herself as she scurried toward the door and whispered, "I'm sorry." The other technician left too, so I tumbled off the table and went to look at the picture that was still on the screen. I didn't see anything unusual. It just looked like a blurry negative of a skinny baby. I looked down at my stomach and rubbed it as I said, "I think we're in trouble."

After the amniocentesis, my husband and I went back to the hospital to get the test results. The doctor said, as if he were reading from a textbook, "Trisomy 18 is a genetic disorder that always involves profound mental retardation and severe disfigurements." Then he said the words that still echo inside a tiny zipped pocket of my heart, "Your baby's condition is usually incompatible with life. Most women in your position—in order to spare themselves unnecessary anguish—just get an abortion. We can schedule yours for tomorrow morning."

I wasn't able to speak. I stopped breathing. I felt like I was drowning. I wanted to drift down into cool dark water and die. Ron and I left the office without a word.

That afternoon, I prayed, *Lord, I believe abortion is wrong, but I don't want to go through, "unnecessary anguish." I don't have the strength to fall in love with a baby who's going to die.*

I kept saying it, even before I meant it: "I choose to love this baby with all my heart." I willed my words into actions. In faith, I moved my hands as I timidly caressed my stomach. In faith, I moved my lips as I mouthed the words, *I love you.* No sound came out. I kept repeating the phrase until my brain finally found the secret passageway to my heart, and I was free to taste the bittersweet tears of loving a child who would never love me in return.

My mother told me, "Try not to think about the future. Your baby is alive today—be alive with him. Treasure every moment."

I talked to him, sang lullabies to him, and prayed for him. I gave him gentle massages through my skin. I knew I had to do my best mothering in whatever time I had with him—even before he was born.

Four months later, we met little Timmy face to face. The nurse covered his fragile, twenty-ounce body in a soft blue blanket and matching cap. His heart monitor beeped an unsteady greeting as she handed him to me.

His beautiful little rosebud-mouth surprised me. It was an oasis of perfection. We held our emotions in check, knowing we had to pour a lifetime of love into a minuscule cup. Ron and I took turns rocking him as we repeatedly told him, "We love you, Timmy." He never opened his eyes. His heartbeat got slower and slower and then, reluctantly, stopped.

We introduced him to his heavenly Father: Lord, here is our son. Thank You for the gift of his precious life and for the privilege of being his parents. We release him into Your care.

Then we cried.

I looked at my neighbor's tear-stained face and said, "I had this ring made a few days after Timmy's birth. I drew a picture of what I wanted, told the jeweler why I wanted it, and he worked late into the night to have it for me the next day." She looked closer as I explained the design.

"The ring has two curved bands of gold. The longer one symbolizes my husband's arm and the smaller band represents mine. Our 'arms' are holding a small, lavender alexandrite—Timmy's birthstone. There are thirteen tiny diamonds; one precious stone for each minute that he was alive. I wear it on my 'baby' finger every day and night. He's always with me."

She was silent for a long time, and finally said, "You should be the only person in the world to wear that ring. I won't copy your design."

As I hugged her I knew that what I told her was true—Timmy would always be with me, on my baby finger and in my heart.

# $\mathscr{A}$ GOOD DAY

## HEIDI SANDERS

*O LORD, I have come to you for protection; don't let me be put*

*to shame. Rescue me, for you always do what is right. Bend down*

*and listen to me; rescue me quickly. Be for me a great rock of safety,*

*a fortress where my enemies cannot reach me.*

PSALM 31:1-2 NLT

*Today's going to be a good day,* I try to convince myself. I wipe off my baby's face and hands and mop up the spilled cereal milk from his high-chair tray. Things have been difficult for me since I found out I was pregnant again. I can't help remembering the complications I had with my last pregnancy. And this time I'm even more tired and weak. I have three kids to care for, but some days I feel as if I can barely care for myself.

My husband, Aaron, tries to reassure and comfort me. He is doing the dishes and telling me I worry too much. "Relax, Heidi," he says. "Ask God for help and then just trust Him."

With that thought, I stroke my rounded belly and pour a cup

of tea. *Today will be a good day,* I repeat to myself.

Loud banging on the front door startles me. Aaron and I look at each other and wonder who it could be. We were hoping to spend the afternoon together, to savor our family time. The children are gathering around my knees, and Aaron shushes them. "Let's try to be really quiet. We can make believe we're asleep or out on a walk," my husband says. I sympathize with his frustration, but something inside of me tells me that we should respond. "It could be important, Aaron," I say.

I peek out the door and see our neighbor Frank, his face red and hands trembling. His wife is pregnant too, only she was much farther along than I am—almost to full term. "Heidi, come quick," he cries. "Carol's having her baby. And the midwife's not here yet!"

Although I have given birth to three children myself, that doesn't make me an expert! I have no medical knowledge or training. But again, something inside of me tells me that Carol needs me, at least until the midwife gets there.

I slip on my shoes and run out the door without even saying good-bye to Aaron and the boys. Climbing into Frank's pickup, I push his tools aside and lean back against the seat. My heart is beating as fast as Frank is talking. I need to calm down if I'm going to be of help. God, let me know just what to do.

Aaron's words rang in my ears, *Ask God for help and then just trust Him.* I am trying to trust, but my body is tense.

"I have everything on the midwife's list," Frank says as we pull into his driveway. We race inside. "Let me know if you need anything else," he says.

"Sure," I answer, and then it hits me. Frank plans on waiting in the other room until the ordeal is over! I'm in this alone. What have I gotten myself into?

I find Carol in the den, stretched out on an old recliner, tears streaming down her face. "It's going to be okay," I say, kneeling next to her.

"The baby's coming," she answers, her eyes huge, terrified. "Now!"

Carol groans. I can tell she's in hard labor. How am I going to do this alone?

"I have to push," Carol screams. "Can I push?" How do I know? Fighting back panic, I force myself to focus. *Trust God,* I remember. "No, you can't push yet," I hear myself say. In my mind I hear Aaron saying, *Relax, Heidi, God is with you.*

I rack my brain for every bit of information or memory about childbirth. "I have to push," Carol gasps.

"No, don't push, just breathe," I tell her. I breathe with her. "Let it out slowly." I want to wait for the midwife, but I see the dark hair of the baby's head crowning. "On the next contraction, you can push, but stay in control," I say. I apply a little pressure to the baby's head with the palm of my hand to keep it from plunging out too fast for me to hold on. The baby slides against my wrist and lands safely in my arms. "It's a boy!" A sharp cry pierces the air.

Frank runs into the room. A big weary smile illuminates Carol's perspiration-covered face. I slowly straighten up, my legs throbbing after kneeling for so long. Carefully I place the slippery baby on Carol's chest and wipe the sweat from her brow.

The midwife shows up just after I cut the cord. I call Aaron to check on the boys. I kiss Carol good-bye and tell her I'll call her in the morning.

"I want to thank you for everything," Frank says as he drops me off at home.

"Anytime," I say.

Aaron greets me at the door and gently holds me in his arms. We watch the sunset disappear on the horizon. Carol and her new baby are probably sleeping soundly by now. A small foot pushes at the inside of my rib cage, and I no longer feel afraid. I had learned a valuable lesson that day—I had listened to God's voice speaking to me, obeyed what He told me to do, and He took control of the situation. Trust God. Today was a good day.

# *O*UT LOUD

## LAURA L. SMITH

*Trust in the LORD with all thine heart;*

*and lean not unto thine own understanding.*

*In all thy ways acknowledge him, and he shall direct thy paths.*

PROVERBS 3:5-6

Brett looked as gray and blank as a computer monitor that had been turned off. I could tell the response to my usual, "How was your day?" on that chilly November evening would not be his typical warm answer. As the Vice President of Business Development for the latest and greatest Internet start up company, he was always mentally wired when he arrived home from a day in the high-tech world. Today was different.

"Our CEO gathered the troops into the conference room after lunch," Brett spoke deliberately, like a robot. "Despite everyone's eagerness, no one was prepared for what he said. 'We didn't receive our next round of funding,' the CEO explained. 'Everyone needs to pack up their personal belongings.

Our doors are closing today.' "

It took a moment for Brett's story to sink in. Careerelite.com was no more. That meant my husband no longer had a job. It meant a blow to his ego and a sense of emptiness in his life. It meant we no longer had an income.

"Are you okay?" I asked.

"I think so," he replied, sinking into the sofa. "I mean, we knew this was a possibility. A new company is always a bit of a gamble."

What's an out-of-work dot-com guy with a pregnant wife and a two-year-old child to support to do? We had enough money to get by for a couple of months, but then what?

"In high school I dreamed of becoming a teacher, but I never pursued it because of the low salaries," Brett sighed. "Maybe now is the time to make a career change?" he asked more than he stated.

Brett began to think about teaching at a college where he could share his business knowledge and guide young adults to moral choices as they entered the "real world"—to make a positive impact on others instead of just making more money. But how would an unemployed Internet entrepreneur with no teaching experience go about becoming an instructor at a university?

Brett called a friend he had kept in close contact with from our college days. This friend had become a professor and gave Brett some incredible feedback. The professor felt Brett would be a gifted teacher, and he even suspected there would be an opening in Brett's major in the upcoming fall at their alma mater.

But there was a catch. Brett didn't have a PhD. The vast majority of American universities do not allow anyone without a doctorate to teach in their business schools. But the job Brett's faculty friend had mentioned was an "instructor" position—designed for people with MBAs and real-world experience, just like Brett, to share their knowledge with eager students.

We began to play the "what if" game about the situation: "What if" a position really did become available in the fall? "What if" Brett had the opportunity to interview for it? "What if" he got the job? Based on those fantastical assumptions, our brains kicked into gear. Becoming an instructor would require relocating from Atlanta, a city of over 3.5 million people, to Oxford, Ohio—population 12,000. We would have to sell our house, pay for a move, and buy a new home. We would also have to leave the family and friends we had known for ten years and also give up the unbeatable climate. And, most distressing of all, Brett would be forced to take an 80 percent pay cut!

But on the other hand, he would be fulfilling a childhood dream to teach. We would be living within two hours of both sets of our parents. We would be returning to our alma mater, where we had met and where so many beautiful memories were formed.

At church the following Sunday, our pastor, Father Al, gave a sermon on the passage of Scripture in which Jesus calls His disciples. They were asked to leave their homes, their friends and family, and their possessions to follow Him and to do His will.

Father Al's sermon concluded with a short story relaying what might have taken place when Jesus returned to Heaven after His resurrection: The angels all eagerly gathered around Jesus and asked how He planned to continue the expansion of His Kingdom on earth now that He was back in Heaven. The Lord replied, "I've assembled twelve vagrants to carry out My mission."

The angels stood in shock, but didn't want to insult Jesus. They pleaded, "With all due respect, Lord, what if these men fail? What then?"

Jesus answered, "I have no other plan."

If Jesus had enough faith in a group of fishermen and tax collectors to spread Christianity throughout the world, surely He would give us the gifts we needed to carry out the mission He had in mind for us. The impact of our eloquent pastor's words and the relevance they had to our current decision left wet, salty stains on both sets of our cheeks.

Our material possessions had been a major sticking point in our decision-making process. We were willing to make sacrifices, but reducing our existing income by four-fifths was more than a sacrifice—it was an extreme obstacle! We, too, would need to give up our home, some relationships, and the luxuries of Brett's corporate job to follow God's plan.

On Wednesday of that week Brett got the call. The head of the marketing department at the business school wanted to interview him. Was this too good to be true or, too difficult?

On Friday, I questioned no more. I was taking a walk at our neighborhood park, pushing our daughter, Maddie, in her stroller. I was breathing in the crisp air and the scent of moist earth. In a rare moment of silence I prayed to God for an answer to our dilemma. Should we follow what truly seemed like His call to a small town and a new seemingly more humble life, or should we be less spontaneous and more responsible by earning a stable income to support our daughter, our unborn baby, and ourselves? Didn't we have a commitment as parents to provide for our children? Shouldn't we take care of ourselves by maintaining a strong enough financial position to save for the unforeseeable future?

As my thoughts whirled through my head, a voice boomed, *Go to Oxford!*

I stopped the stroller. Nobody was in sight besides Maddie

and I, and the strong steady voice had not come from her small lips. It had seemed to come from thin air, and there was no doubt in my mind or heart that it was the Lord talking to me.

So just like the prophets in the Bible, I tested this miracle. I prayed again.

*Do You really want us to go, I mean...*

Before I could get out any of my reasons why this was such a difficult decision, the voice came again, *You heard me. Go to Oxford.*

His distinct reply contrasted so greatly with my wavering pleas and rationalizations. God made no excuses or explanations. His answer was simple.

As soon as I got home I shared my story with Brett, and he believed me, but since he didn't get to hear God speaking firsthand, he still had doubts.

The next day, he was cleaning out his desk and came across one of his favorite poems, "The Road Not Taken," by Robert Frost. He put a copy in his briefcase to remind him that perhaps teaching, taking the road "less traveled by" would "make all the difference." The following week he went to Oxford for his interview. He stopped for a cup of coffee prior to his meeting. On the chalkboard of the cafe, right there among the sorority and fraternity letters and the joke of the day, someone had written, in its entirety, Robert Frost's wise words.

Brett got the job, and we are moving to Ohio next month.

God speaks to us in so many ways. Through people we meet, things we hear and read, feelings, and impressions. These everyday life occurrences, a sermon, a poem, a contact with an old friend, are not coincidences.

Listen for God. He is talking to you. He is guiding you away from the ways of the world and toward the ways of His Kingdom. This Kingdom journey is on a road less traveled by the common man. You won't always understand why you are on this path, or where it is leading, but God does. Trust His plan for your life and follow it. You'll be glad you did.

# MIRACLE ON A SUNDAY AFTERNOON

## LAROSE KARR

*He will command his angels concerning you*

*to guard you in all your ways.*

PSALM 91:11 NIV

While traveling on an unfamiliar highway in Nebraska, my son approached a small curve in the road. Speeding with the cruise control set at seventy miles per hour, he leaned over to tune the radio and in a second's time lost control of his small truck. It veered into the opposite lane, striking a mile marker, and then spun completely around. Finally it became airborne, flipped upside down, and then crashed to the ground.

Nothing short of a miracle occurred for my family on that beautiful fall day. Brett said that as the events unfolded— almost in slow motion—he knew he would live. He knew! The truck came to rest on a slight incline on the side of the road with the cab flattened, level with the truck bed. The windshield was shattered and mangled but not broken out. Coming to rest on the small hill is what saved him: The force of the crash created a V-shape on the roof of the passenger side, which in turn created a slight oval cave above his head.

After the vehicle landed, Brett could not breathe. Even with the windows rolled up, dust filled the air inside the vehicle. He thought, *I am not going to die now—not after I survived the crash!* Brett was hanging upside down and held in place by the seatbelt, but he finally managed to unhook the belt, roll down the window, and slide out on his back.

Two vehicles stopped to help, and one passerby provided a cell phone for Brett to call his dad. But when the call came through, the connection was bad, and my husband, Larry, was so upset that he forgot to write the details down. Panic-stricken, Larry could only recall that Brett was on Highway 23 in Nebraska, and he'd been involved in a rollover that totaled his truck. A family came along and stayed with our son until the sheriff arrived.

Meanwhile Larry and I jumped in the car and left our home in Colorado, heading for Nebraska. When we reached the state line, trouble surfaced as Larry couldn't remember the name of the town where the accident had taken place. We found ourselves examining every skid mark on the road to determine if it was our son's accident site.

I began to pray, *Father, please lead us to our son. Lord,*

*take us right to Brett, wherever he may be.* We traveled through several small towns and literally almost missed Grant, Nebraska. On the outer edge of the town, we decided to turn around and go back to find a payphone, thinking that perhaps our son had called home. We stopped on the main street, and as I raised my hand to place coins in the phone, our prayers were suddenly answered. A sheriff's car pulled up with Brett inside! We discovered later that Brett had been on the opposite side of the street with the deputy, right where the tow truck had deposited his vehicle. The accident had occurred just thirty miles east of Grant!

The Lord knew exactly where our son was, and He led us directly to him. When we all got to the hospital, although he was very sore, Brett checked into the emergency room with only a bruise on his eye and cut on his eyelid.

When I eventually viewed the mangled wreckage that had been his truck, I said, "Brett, you know that angels were with you." You see, Brett had lost a friend the previous week in a similar accident while he was traveling only forty-five miles per hour. His friend was not wearing a seatbelt. Distraught and grieving the loss of his friend, Brett had been easily distracted that day, and his accident occurred as a result.

We buried Brett's friend the following week. It was a reflective time for me as I comforted the grieving family, all the while knowing that it could have been my son too. As I listened to the pastor's eulogy, in my mother's heart I painfully understood that this young man whose life had ended would always be entwined with my son's. His friend is gone, but Brett is still alive for whatever purpose God has yet to unfold.

Our son survived his accident just as he knew he would. Thank God for the lessons learned on the unfamiliar road my son took. Praise God for an answer to a mother's fervent prayer and the reflection of life in the midst of trouble. Thank God for the miracle on a Sunday afternoon.

#  LITTLE REASSURANCE

## WENDY DUNHAM

*Have no fear of sudden disaster or of the ruin that overtakes the wicked, for*

*the LORD will be your confidence and will keep your foot from being snared.*

PROVERBS 3:25-26 NIV

It's 1:10 A.M. in the morning, and I hear my daughter's voice as it breaks the silence of the night.

"Mom," I can hear her softly call from upstairs. Several seconds pass in silence.

"Mom?" she calls out again, only a bit louder this time.

I slowly roll out of bed knowing it's not an emergency or I would have heard yelling instead. I stumble through the nighttime maze of furniture and manage to reach the stairway. Standing at the base, I look up and see Erin's seven-year-old silhouette of "baby-doll jammies" and shoulder-length braids.

"What's the matter, Erin?" I question.

"I have to go to the bathroom, but there's a moth in there and he's scaring me."

"It's alright," I reassure her. "He won't bother you...he's sleeping."

Having no concept of the time passed since she had gone to bed, Erin asked, "And what are you doing?"

"I was sleeping, Erin."

She continues with her questions. "But did you already check on me?" (One of my many nighttime duties).

"No," I explain, "Daddy checked on you. I'm very tired."

"Oh," she said, "he's home from his meeting already?"

"Yes, he's home...and he's sleeping too."

"Oh, okay, Mom. I love you." Then with innocence, she blows me a kiss, and her silhouette braids bounce away.

I backtrack through the darkened rooms and crawl back in bed. I can't sleep. As the conversation with Erin replays in my mind, I begin to understand a little better how my relationship to my daughter reflects God's relationship to me. I imagine how I must appear to Him.

"God?" I whisper, "are You there?"

*Yes, I'm here,* He answers. *I'm always here.*

"What are You doing?"

*I'm watching over You...one of my many jobs.*

"Oh," I say, "thanks, God. That's nice to know, because sometimes it gets a little scary down here. Good night, God. I love You."

He reassures me, *I love you, too.*

I smile to myself, and drift back to sleep.

Isn't it reassuring to know that our Heavenly Father is watching over us all the time? He never sleeps, never takes a nap, never takes a coffee break or even a two-week vacation.

Knowing that, I can have a confidence and a peace that overcomes all my fears.

# THE RICHEST FAMILY AT CHURCH

## SALLY ANN SMITH

*"I assure you," he said, "this poor widow has given more than all the rest of them. For they have given a tiny part of their surplus, but she, poor as she is, has given everything she has."*

LUKE 21:3-4 NLT

I'll never forget Easter, 1946. I was fourteen, my little sister Ocy twelve, and my older sister Darlene sixteen. We lived at home with our mother, and the four of us knew what it was to do without many things.

My dad had died five years before, leaving Mom with seven school-age kids to raise and no money. By 1946, my older sisters were married and my brothers had left home.

A month before Easter, the pastor of our church announced that a special Easter offering would be taken to help a poor family. He asked everyone to save and give sacrificially.

When we got home, we talked about what we could do. We

decided to buy fifty pounds of potatoes and live on them for a month. This would allow us to save $20 of our grocery money for the offering.

Then we thought that if we kept our electric lights turned out as much as possible and didn't listen to the radio, we'd save money on that month's electric bill. Darlene got as many house and yard cleaning jobs as possible, and both of us baby-sat for everyone we could. For fifteen cents, we could buy enough cotton loops to make three pot holders to sell for $1. We made $20 on pot holders.

That month was one of the best of our lives. Every day we counted the money to see how much we had saved. At night we'd sit in the dark and talk about how the poor family was going to enjoy having the money the church would give them. We had about eighty people in church, so we figured that whatever amount of money we had to give, the offering would surely be twenty times that much. After all, every Sunday the pastor had reminded everyone to save for the sacrificial offering.

The day before Easter, Ocy and I walked to the grocery store and got the manager to give us three crisp $20 bills and one $10 bill for all our change. We ran all the way home to show Mom and Darlene. We had never had so much money before. That night we were so excited we could hardly sleep. We didn't care that we wouldn't have new clothes for Easter;

we had $70 for the sacrificial offering. We could hardly wait to go to church!

On Sunday morning, rain was pouring down. We didn't own an umbrella, and the church was over a mile from our home, but it didn't seem to matter how wet we got. Darlene had cardboard in her shoes to fill the holes. The cardboard came apart and her feet got wet. But we sat in church proudly. I heard some teenagers talking about the Smith girls having on their old dresses. I looked at them in their new clothes, and yet I felt so rich.

When the sacrificial offering was taken, we were sitting in the second row from the front. Mom put in the $10 bill, and each of us girls put in a $20. As we walked home after church, we sang all the way. At lunch Mom had a surprise for us. She had bought a dozen eggs, and we had boiled Easter eggs with our fried potatoes!

Late that afternoon the minister drove up in his car. Mom went to the door, talked with him for a moment, and then came back with an envelope in her hand. We asked what it was, but she didn't say a word. She opened the envelope, and out fell a bunch of money. There were three crisp $20 bills, one $10 and seventeen $1 bills.

Mom put the money back in the envelope. We didn't talk, we just sat and stared at the floor. We'd gone from feeling like millionaires to feeling like poor white trash.

We kids had had such a happy life that we felt sorry for anyone who didn't have a life like ours and a house full of brothers and sisters and other kids visiting constantly.

We thought it was fun to share silverware and see whether we got the fork or the spoon that night. We had two knives, which we passed around to whoever needed them.

I knew we didn't have a lot of things that other people had but I had never thought we were poor.

That Easter Day I found out we were. The minister had brought us the money for the poor family, so we must be poor.

I didn't like being poor. I looked at my dress and worn-out shoes and felt so ashamed that I didn't want to go back to church. Everyone there probably already knew we were poor! I thought about school. I was in the ninth grade and at the top of my class of over 100 students. I wondered if the kids at school knew we were poor. I decided I could quit school since I had finished the eighth grade. That was all the law required at that time.

We sat in silence for a long time. Then it got dark, and we went to bed. All that week, we girls went to school and came home, and no one talked much. Finally on Saturday, Mom asked us what we wanted to do with the money. What did poor people do with money? We didn't know. We'd never known we were poor.

We didn't want to go to church on Sunday, but Mom said

we had to. Although it was a sunny day, we didn't talk on the way. Mom started to sing, but no one joined in, and she only sang one verse.

At church we had a missionary speaker. He talked about how churches in Africa made buildings out of sun-dried bricks, but they needed money to buy roofs. He said $100 would put a roof on a church. The minister said, "Can't we all sacrifice to help these poor people?"

We looked at each other and smiled for the first time in a week. Mom reached in her purse and pulled out the envelope. She passed it to Darlene, Darlene gave it to me, and I handed it to Ocy. Ocy put it in the offering.

When the offering was counted, the minister announced that it was a little over $100. The missionary was excited. He hadn't expected such a large offering from our small church. He said, "You must have some rich people in this church."

Suddenly, it struck us! We had given $87 of that "little over $100." We were the rich family at the church! Hadn't the missionary said so?

As I grew older, our decision that day to place the money we had been given back in the offering stuck with me. When we followed God's way and gave the best that we had, we realized we had riches far greater than anything this world's money could buy.

# ℒORD, BRING HER A CHRISTIAN FRIEND

## SUSANNE SCHEPPMANN

*The effectual fervent prayer of a righteous man availeth much.*

JAMES 5:16

"I hate you!" she yelled as the door slammed behind her. Sighing, I recalled the ten long years I had prayed for the Lord to bring my stepdaughter, Erin, a Christian friend. Until now, she had lived with her mother in another state. Because of the distance, our influence as Christian parents seemed insignificant. My husband, Mark, and I had longed to raise her in our Christian home. I imagined the great impact our home would have on her life. Yet, I doubted we would ever have the opportunity. At sixteen and a junior in high school, it was unlikely she would come to live with us. So what could I do? I prayed for God to place a Christian friend into Erin's life to win her to Christ.

I prayed. I wrote in my prayer journal of my desires and

concerns regarding Erin, but I saw few positive results. In fact, just the opposite of what I was praying for seemed to happen. We discovered Erin was getting involved in some questionable relationships. She had started down a path of self-destruction. I began to question if God had even heard my prayers for Erin.

Then suddenly on a December night, we received a crisis call from Erin's mother. Erin had locked herself in the bathroom, threatening suicide over an inappropriate relationship that had been exposed. Mark immediately requested that Erin come and stay with us, at least for the Christmas vacation. He left within the hour to be with her, pack her bags, and drive her back to our home.

Erin arrived angry and full of rebellion. Her long hair hung around tear-swollen eyes. She did not want to stay with us. She didn't try to hide her emotions or feelings. Turmoil decorated our home rather than a pleasant Christmas atmosphere. Little did I know that I had just begun one of the most difficult seasons of my adult life.

With her mother's grudging consent, Erin came to live with us on a full-time basis. As a blended family adjusting to a new member, we felt as if we were being pureed in a blender. We fought, we cried, and we prayed. I began to wonder if we would survive!

Family counseling brought small relief. The counselor simply stated the obvious: "Erin despises the rules of your household." Obsessed with "the love of her life," she snuck phone calls and even short visits to see him. No matter how we tried to stop the relationship, Erin discovered ways to stay involved.

She manipulated. I manipulated. We argued constantly. I determined I would be the Christian mother she desperately needed, but did not want. I would win this battle at any cost. Erin would obey our Christian standards. Our home grew rigid with rules. The plaque above the door that read, "As for me and my house, we will serve the Lord," became not my motherly motto, but my demand.

My faith ran low in believing any change could occur. But although my faith faltered, my prayers continued, still echoing the refrain, *Lord, bring her a Christian friend.*

The night she yelled, "I hate you!" I curled up in bed, discouraged and exhausted. Questions surfaced: *Lord, do You hear me at all?* I picked up my prayer journal from the nightstand and thumbed through the pages of the past few months. Over and over the record of my prayers cried, Lord, bring her a Christian friend! Suddenly, the answer to my prayer became clear. God showed me that He wanted me to be the friend who would point her to Him.

I had missed the answer that was right in front of me. God's plan provided for a friend for Erin, not the insistent, intolerant stepmom I had become.

Suddenly I began to work diligently to win her confidence and trust. I begged her to forgive me. She graciously forgave, and we began a new relationship—a relationship based on a friendship that had the blessing of God upon it.

Our home became a haven for Erin to feel accepted and wanted. We even grew to enjoy each other's company. Slowly, her behavior began to change. She started to conform to the standards of our home. And eventually, I had the honor of seeing her accept Jesus Christ as her personal Savior and be baptized shortly afterward. Erin ended up living with us until she graduated from high school two years later.

Was it easy? No. Does Erin still struggle with life? Absolutely! Do I still pray for her? Yes, indeed! I know God does hear and answer my prayers, but He may surprise and challenge me with His answers. I learned that when I pray, I might become the answer to my own prayer.

# DANCING TO A DIFFERENT TUNE

## KATHRYN LAY

*They sang a new song with these words:*

*"You are worthy to take the scroll and break its seals and open it.*

*For you were killed, and your blood has ransomed people for*

*God from every tribe and language and people and nation.*

REVELATION 5:9 NLT

"I LOOK UPON THE WORLD AS MY PARISH."

*John Wesley*

I watch with pride as the other children pull my daughter into the dancing circle of two hundred adults, teens, and children. Michelle's fair hair and skin stands out in contrast to the dark-haired children with their glittering dresses.

But they are her friends, despite their differences, despite their countries of origin, despite anything others might say. They welcome her into their world. And she welcomes them into hers.

It had been a busy weekend, a culturally eclectic time for our family. We had enjoyed a cool, rainy Saturday shivering in a gazebo, tapping our feet with strangers while our seven-year-old daughter and other children danced and skipped to lively Irish jigs and folksongs.

The very next evening my husband, daughter, and I were invited to share the wedding celebration of two of our Kurdish students from our English As a Second Language classes. We are three of ten Americans in a crowd of five hundred Kurdish refugees, feeling greatly honored to have been invited to this celebration. We are careful and conscious of their customs, not wanting to offend, but it isn't long before the joy of the moment and the acceptance we receive draw us into their world.

For seven years we've watched the "No Longer Strangers" ministry grow from providing simple English classes, to helping refugees with problems and citizenship, to becoming their friends, and finally to witnessing to them about God's love through Jesus' life, death, and resurrection.

Sometimes the barriers are difficult. Our newfound Muslim friends will happily talk about politics, family, customs, traditions, and food. But approaching the subject of Christ is often met with distrust or arguments.

I watch my daughter dance with the other children. They stop only long enough to weave a game of chase through the tables until they finally press into the crowd waiting for the first pieces of wedding cake.

At night, she prays for her new friends from around the world. She knows our goals are threefold: to help these people, to show them that we love them, and most importantly, to share God's love. For her and the other children, politics are unimportant; the truth comes easily for them.

Michelle is comfortable wherever we are: the dinners in the homes of Vietnamese friends, the chicken feet she brags to everyone that she ate at the home of two Chinese students, the Thanksgiving celebrations filled with friends and food from Mexico, Korea, Iraq, Kurdistan, and Taiwan. In each case, she quickly befriends the children, while we adults have to work hard at understanding one another.

I've watched my daughter joyfully dance to African songs she's seen on Sesame Street or when visiting with our writer friend from Africa as he spins his tales of friendship and adventure from his own country. But because my own father had no tolerance for those who were different than him, my own acceptances don't come as easy as my daughter's.

Yet God has given us a ministry to the world, right in our own backyard. Friends often shake their heads at the stories we tell of such weddings, New Years Eve parties, or other celebrations.

"How weird," a friend comments.

But weird is in the eye of the beholder.

My daughter, on the other hand, sees the differences as exciting, the challenges as fun, the barriers as simply walls to climb over and discover what waits beyond.

Is Michelle learning to dance her way into cultural understanding? What a wonderful thought!

It's a simple thing to say that we should dance with, rather than around, our views of other cultures. But perhaps, as my daughter dances and eats and sits entranced with the variety of cultural differences around her, she and other children like her will grow up with a view of the joy of learning about those who are different. And they may discover that they are not so very different after all.

After recently moving to an older part of town, hoping to fit in and really get to know our students who come to the classes offered at our church, my husband and I found that we were quickly accepted and looked at as friends. In a time when many neighbors put up fences both physically and emotionally, I've been amazed at the joy our neighbors from Mexico have in bringing us tamales for Christmas.

Again we are invited to a Kurdish wedding celebration where we adults compliment the beautiful dresses the women are wearing. We clap with the music, struggling to shout over the noise and make ourselves understood, while holding babies and taking care not to offend.

My daughter continues to dance. Other children join the circle, hands clasping even as they talk in a language Michelle cannot understand.

I watch her in pride and a little bit of envy and pray...*Lord, please let them save a dance for me.*

# ℬE NOT AFRAID

## STACI STALLINGS

*Let not your heart be troubled, neither let it be afraid.*

JOHN 14:27

Fear is one thing. Helpless anxiety is another.

Fear heightens your awareness, makes you ready to fight— to take on the aggressor and win.

Helpless anxiety, on the other hand, saps every ounce of energy and makes you think that nothing you do will make any difference. Helpless anxiety wraps around you like a wet blanket. It weighs on you, takes the breath right out of you. It's a horrible feeling to experience.

That's where I was—wrapped in helpless anxiety—as I sat in the darkened church, feeling empty and alone. My husband sat beside me, holding my hand, but that didn't seem to help. Nor did it change the fact that our baby was six miles away lying in an incubator, fighting for her life. Born three months early, her tiny body was covered in a mass of tubes and wires.

Her legs were the size of my husband's finger, and her tiny little hand couldn't even get all the way around my finger.

And I was helpless to do anything to make her better.

Sure, the doctors told me I was lucky that I had taken such good care of myself, that because of my good health, she was developed even beyond the twenty-five weeks she should have been. But I didn't feel like much of a hero. I felt like I had let down this little one who was counting on me. The should-haves and could-haves ran around in my head, constantly bumping into one another and tripping over themselves, constantly reminding me of my guilt. That night, as I listened to what was supposed to be an uplifting sermon, I didn't feel very uplifted. In fact, I felt more depressed than I ever had in my life.

Then the soloist began to sing a song from my past. I knew the words by heart although I suddenly wondered if I had ever really understood them. I tried to sing, to get the words to come out of my mouth, but my heart just hurt too much. Instead of words, tears began to flow as God whispered to me through the words of the song: "Be not afraid. I go before you always. Come follow Me, and I will give you rest."

Be not afraid? How could I not be afraid? Fear was the only thing I could feel. I wanted to do something. I wanted to make things better. I wanted to go back and a do a hundred million things differently so that we wouldn't be in this place, praying for my daughter's survival. And yet, God was telling me not to be afraid.

For the first time since the whole ordeal had begun nearly a month before, I cried. I didn't want to, but I couldn't stop the tears from flowing down my cheeks. As the singing continued on, about knowing God is with you through it all, God spoke through that person to me, giving me comfort in my hour of greatest need.

In minutes the song was over. I wiped my face, picked up my courage, and marched forward—with a hope that God did indeed have a plan in mind, that he would be faithful to His promise that He had not given me a spirit of fear; but of power and love.

Over the course of the next month, slowly but surely, my daughter gained weight. One agonizing gram at a time. At one point we even threatened to stuff her diaper with quarters (each weighed one gram) so that she could reach the magic number—1812 grams—4 pounds, so we could take her home. Although at the time it seemed an eternity, in retrospect it doesn't seem like it took all that long. Two months to be exact. A full month less than the doctors had warned it would take. Then one wonderful September day, we got to take our perfectly healthy baby home for good.

Less than a year later, I stood with my baby girl in my arms in that same church, and suddenly that familiar music started once again: "Be not afraid... I go before you always...." I looked down at my beautiful girl, and the tears started rolling down my face once more. Hugging my baby close to me, I could only sing with my heart because my tears choked out the words.

Even today, seven years and a hundred scraped knees later, when the notes of that song play in my mind, I am reminded, to the depths of my soul, that God is indeed here with me. In my most terrifying moments, He is by my side. More than that, He can see all and holds my future securely in His hands. And so, as a wise man once said, "All I have seen teaches me to trust Him for all I have not seen."

Because of one talented songwriter whom I'm sure I will never meet, I now understand that we can all "be not afraid...."

# $\mathscr{G}$OD PUT A SONG ON MY LIPS

## NANCY GIBBS

*Sing unto him a new song...for the word of the LORD is right;*

*and all his works are done in truth.*

PSALM 33:3-4

I had celebrated my seventeenth birthday just a month before I became a wife. My father and I walked down the aisle with our arms intertwined. I knew that Daddy wasn't certain that his little girl should grow up that early, but he didn't try to stop me. He let me make my own decision regarding my future.

A year quickly passed by. I discovered a new role in life. I became a mother, not only to one baby boy, but to two. God blessed me with twins. At eighteen years of age, I had my hands full. I grew up very quickly. My friends were going to senior proms and participating in graduation exercises, but I graduated almost a year early. My diploma was sent to me in the mail. I never wore a cap and gown.

I spent my days cleaning house, washing diapers, and cooking. The nights were long, as both babies vied for my attention. Many times I felt lonely in the confines of our house. My husband worked faithfully, but also had fun with his friends just as religiously. He didn't spend much time at home and as my father feared, the marriage was short-lived.

I managed okay most of the time. I was mature enough to understand that things would eventually change and that with time, life would become a little easier. As a child, I didn't attend church, so I didn't realize that I could turn to God. While I was convinced that there was a God, I was not certain that He cared about me. But the love I had for my children kept me going.

One night in particular, I was home alone with my two small babies. They were both desperately ill. We had gone to see the doctor that day, but the medication he prescribed didn't seem to be helping. Both boys continued to run a high fever, and neither of them would let me put them down.

Even though I was exhausted, I realized that there would be no sleep for me that night. I kept fresh washcloths in a bucket of cool water beside the rocking chair to keep them cool. I rocked and washed their foreheads until I began to cry.

But then the words of an encouraging Christian song came

to my mind. I began to sing aloud. At first, I whispered the words. Then my song became louder and louder as I rocked with a baby in each arm. Soon, my boys fell peacefully asleep. Each time I paused, they stirred, and so I sang until I finally drifted off to sleep myself in the wee hours of the morning.

I awoke the next morning to the sun shining through the curtains and down upon my face. I was holding a baby tightly in each arm. Their foreheads were cool, and they awoke feeling much better. The song I sang helped the three of us survive that difficult night. And yet, for some reason I could not remember the melody or even the words of the song. I simply remembered singing until I drifted off to sleep.

God eventually sent a wonderful man into my life. Roy is a minister, and he not only fell in love with me, but he fell in love with my sons, as well. Two months after we were married, we began adoption procedures, and he became the legal father of my two precious little boys. About ten months after that, we welcomed our daughter into the world. Our family has been tied together by a love that came from God.

Roy and I began to serve in churches together. I loved my new life dearly. One Sunday morning, I heard a song that seemed familiar to me. As the song was being sung, my mind went back to the night when I had felt so alone and afraid. It was the very same song that I had been singing the night my boys were so ill. I wondered how I could have even known the words at the time since I didn't attend church, and wasn't serving God. Where had the words come from when I needed them?

But as the vocalist continued to sing about the "Rock of Ages," I knew that God put that song on my lips that night. God had offered the comfort I needed, through a song that I didn't even know.

To this day, almost thirty years later, that song continues to bring joy to my heart and peace to my soul. When times come that I feel afraid or alone, I sing it aloud to myself, it gets me through every trying circumstance that I am facing at the time and helps me focus on the blessed life God has given me.

# THE BIRTHDAY

## KAREN MAJORIS-GARRISON

*Thou wilt make known to me the path of life;*

*in Thy presence is fullness of joy.*

PSALM 16:11

It was my thirty-fifth birthday—a day I had feared. It started with my five-year-old daughter, Abigail, as she bobbed up and down, tugging on my shirt. "Hurry, Mommy, hurry! Blow out the candles!" she had shouted. "And don't forget to say a prayer," she reminded, her brown eyes alight with childish wonder.

"Say a prayer?" her grandmother asked. "What's that about?"

"Silly Grammy!" Abigail laughed, covering her mouth. "We say prayers instead of wishes! It's easy!"

The lights dimmed and the candles flickered. Several witty birthday cards on aging were propped beside the cake. Just last month, my older brother refused to celebrate his fortieth birthday. He had not wanted to be reminded that he was

"WHETHER ONE IS TWENTY, FORTY, OR SIXTY; WHETHER ONE HAS SUCCEEDED, FAILED, OR JUST MUDDLED ALONG; WHETHER YESTERDAY WAS FULL OF SUN OR STORM, OR ONE OF THOSE DULL DAYS WITH NO WEATHER AT ALL, LIFE BEGINS EACH MORNING!"

*Leigh Mitchell Hodges*

getting older. I closed my eyes and breathed deeply. How many people, including myself, did that each year—becoming less and less thankful for the miracle of our lives?

I remembered Psalm 16:11: "Thou wilt make known to me the path of life; in Thy presence is fullness of joy." I asked God to help me stand firm in what He had showed me the previous year during my friend's battle for her life.

My daughter slipped her hand into my pocket, her tiny fingers finding mine. I rubbed her soft skin and sighed, remembering Susie. The mother of two and a wife of twenty years, Susie had been young and vibrant. She had a welcoming grin, a kind heart, and breast cancer. Violently sick from chemotherapy, she had lost her hair and begun a journey of pain and endurance.

Her husband, desperate for a medical breakthrough, had arranged experimental procedures but nothing worked, and Susie's condition worsened. Time passed but Susie refused to give up.

Those who knew her best began to doubt her life-and-death decisions. "Why is she doing this to herself?" they often asked. "She should accept the inevitable: She's going to die. She should stop the treatments and live the rest of her days as best she can. Can't she see that?"

I thought I knew the answer. I had joined together with a

prayer partner, and we had diligently lifted Susie in prayer from the onset of her cancer. Everyone who loved Susie wanted what was best for her. Some chose the "live-your-remaining-days-free-of-medical-services" approach. Others continued helping her find new alternatives. Whatever their advice, Susie never wavered from one path—doing whatever it took to beat the disease. She continued medical treatment though her doctors told her there was little hope.

During Susie's struggle, at night when I cradled my newborn son, I often thought of her family that would be left behind if she died. Maybe it was because of how I loved my own children and husband that her battle affected me so greatly.

Looking at life through Susie's eyes filled me. A new humility and appreciation for each new day surrounded me. When my husband kissed me as he left for work, I'd linger in his arms a little longer. Every night, I'd kneel beside my children's sleeping figures and study their angelic faces—not wanting to take one second for granted. Soon, I began to ache for Susie, and during that time I realized why she'd continued on with such passion.

Susie knew the secret of life. And that secret, simply, was life itself.

She wanted another opportunity to laugh and enjoy her husband's embrace. She wanted to witness her daughter's high-school graduation and her son's first prom. She wanted to see the glory of another sunrise and be in the world when her first grandchild entered it. Life was not a mystery but a miracle. And Susie knew that, right up until the moment when, on a crisp winter day, she died.

"Mama," Abigail said, pointing to the candles. "Hurry, they're melting!"

My husband, holding our precious son, Simeon, caught my eyes from across the table. He kissed the top of Simeon's head and then smiled at me. Butterflies fluttered in my stomach. Those whom I loved most were near.

Because of Susie's zest for life and faith in God, I've never seen birthdays the same way.

Anxiety didn't flood me at my first wrinkles. And since Susie's death, I've never bought an insulting birthday card again. Instead, I've embraced the joys and trials of getting older. After all, each birthday is one more year that I've been able to experience life's many jewels: jewels ranging from my children wrestling with my husband to my being awakened by a bird's morning song.

"Hurry, Mama! Hurry!" Abigail pleaded. "I'll help you blow them out!"

My son giggled, waving his hand at me, and my husband winked. "Let's do it," I told my daughter. We filled our cheeks with air and blew out the candles. The smoke traveled upward.

"Look, Mama! Look!" Abigail shouted, pointing a finger towards the ceiling. "The smoke's carrying your prayer to heaven! It's gonna be answered!"

Bending down, I cupped Abigail's beautiful face. Her eyes were beaming, and I inhaled the sweet scent that was hers alone. "It already has been, honey," I whispered, thanking God for another year. "It already has been."

# NOTHING IS TOO HARD FOR GOD

## JOAN CLAYTON

*"If you have faith as small as a mustard seed, you can say to*
*this mountain, 'Move from here to there' and it will move.*
*Nothing will be impossible for you."*

MATTHEW 17:20 NIV

"Mrs. Clayton," the nurse said breathlessly over the phone, "Lance has been badly burned and is in the hospital. Come quickly!"

Agony gripped my heart. Lance, our son…how we loved him. Just like his daddy, so tall, dark, and handsome, so kind, so gentle…. *Dear God,* I prayed, *be with us.* We need You so! Lance and his wife, Connie, had only been married a few months. Connie was the Godly daughter-in-law I had been praying for.

*Help me,* Lord, *I prayed.* Please give me even stronger faith. Give me peace amidst this terrible storm.

"I sure dread when his mother arrives," I heard one of the nurses say as I approached the emergency room. Emmitt, my husband, stood by Lance's side. Connie held me close. I almost fainted when I looked at Lance. The skin on his arms hung by strings. His face, horribly blistered, was twisted among the red, swollen skin. His cotton T-shirt had melted away and only bare, raw skin remained on his chest. Fear grabbed me by its icy fingers, but I resisted it and felt faith arise. A loud thought in my mind overpowered my threatening panic: *God, this isn't too hard for You!*

Amidst the tears and prayers, I began to hear the story of the accident. Lance had been filling the tractor with butane on my dad's farm, thirty miles from town, when a blinding explosion occurred. His face and arms had been exposed to the full impact of the explosion.

Lance, on fire, rolled over and over in the dirt. We learned later this alone could have caused severe infection. Lance ran to the pickup, but it wouldn't start. That turned out to be a blessing. Being in shock, he would never have made it to town.

*"The tractor! The tractor!"* a still small voice seemed to say. Lance ran to the tractor, started it, and despite the pain, anguish, and shock, began driving blindly. He could hear himself screaming. At breakneck speed, he drove through

pastures and barbed-wire fences until he came upon a large earthen tank, filled with water. He stopped the tractor long enough to submerge himself. This provided some relief and prevented further shock. Lance climbed back onto the tractor, and a few miles later, came upon a little country store, but the store owner's car wouldn't start either. A man "just so happened" to drive up. He also "just so happened" to be a medic from the Vietnam War. He put Lance in his pickup, and they raced to town at one hundred miles an hour. The medic kept talking to Lance, making him answer so that he wouldn't lose consciousness. He had seen many soldiers in a similar condition.

By this time, Emmitt had been contacted. He raced to the hospital, arriving first. When he discovered that Lance and the medic were still on their way, Emmitt immediately left the hospital driving out to meet them, following the state policeman who "just so happened" to be there that day. Later I thought, *How much like our heavenly Father Lance's daddy is. He seeks his own too.*

"Mrs. Clayton?" the doctors were calling from the emergency room. Both Connie and I hurried to the door.

"This is Dr. Jenn," our family doctor was saying. "He has just recently moved to our town and 'just so happens' to be a burn specialist."

"He's a mighty lucky boy," Dr. Jenn said. "He could have

been blinded so easily. He could have been burned much more severely, requiring skin grafts. I cannot tell you right now that there will not be scarring, but we can treat him here. But we must guard him heavily against infection."

I thought of Lance rolling in the dirt and jumping in a dirt tank full of filth and germs, but I made a conscious decision, again forcing myself to pray, *God, this isn't too hard for You!*

As the nurses wheeled Lance to his room, I heard the state patrolman say: "Well, his mother has taken it better than anyone."

At 3 o'clock in the morning of the third day, Emmitt suddenly awakened from a sound sleep and jumped out of bed. "We've got to get to the hospital right now," he exclaimed. "Lance needs us." The Lord was leading again, leading us into intercessory prayer so desperately needed at that hour.

We arrived at the hospital to find Lance in agonizing pain. Since only two at a time with gown and mask could be in Lance's room, Emmitt began his prayer vigil in a chair in the hall, while Connie and I prayed by Lance's bedside.

We had been praying intensely about twenty minutes, when all three of us noticed something unusual. A calm, a peace, a stillness had filled the room. We could almost see the presence of ministering angels. Lance's deep sleep and rhythmic breathing told us that the crisis had passed.

As we were taking Lance home the next day, someone remarked: "Boy, he sure is lucky."

But luck is never coincidence, only God's incident!

Now whenever I reach up to kiss Lance's beautiful face, I think: He's just like his daddy: tall, dark, and handsome. And there is not a single scar!

Lance's life changed forever that day.

"Mom," he said, "Nothing is too hard for God!"

# FORGIVING OUR PRODIGAL SON

## NANETTE THORSEN-SNIPES

*Be ye kind to one another, tenderhearted, forgiving one another,*

*even as God for Christ's sake hath forgiven you.*

EPHESIANS 4:32

The feeling of terror creeps back into my life. But this time it concerns my son, not my former husband. However, the same elements are in place—the gun, the ever-present fear. I sit at my kitchen table and stare at the shards of light dancing in my coffee cup. The coffee is cold now. And the night wears on my nerves as I wait for my son to come home.

I cup my hands around the mug painted brightly with yellow daisies. Years ago, when he was little, my son gave it to me for my birthday. He was always bringing me flowers. Usually they were clenched in his small fist. Sporting a toothless grin, he would cheerfully say, "These are for you, Mama." I would get

> "EVERY PARENT IS AT SOME TIME THE FATHER OF THE UNRETURNED PRODIGAL, WITH NOTHING TO DO BUT KEEP HIS HOUSE OPEN TO HOPE."
>
> *John Ciardi*

down at eye-level with him and hug him tight. Then I would take the wilting wildflowers from his hand and place them in a jelly jar full of water on the kitchen table.

I pour the cold coffee into the sink. My heart breaks as I think back over the past few months. My teenager's anger seemed to erupt over the least thing.

"This bike is no good!" I remember him screaming as he slammed the ten-speed again and again into the ground, until finally it lay in a crumpled heap. He worked so hard in order to buy the bike. But for some reason it didn't operate properly, and he became furious with it.

I cringed at his foul language. And I feared his hostility. Another day, while in an angry rage, he rammed his fist through the basement door and then shattered the mirror in his bedroom. His drinking was becoming a problem, but I didn't know what to do about it.

The anger was so terribly familiar. His father had the same hostility. It seethed for years under a cool exterior until he finally exploded and threatened my life with a loaded gun. My former husband's life ended abruptly. He committed suicide while in jail for threatening his second wife. And now my son had stolen a gun from my bedroom closet, with the same anger boiling inside him.

I watched Jim, my husband, pace the living room floor. His

brow furrowed in worry. "Where is he?" he asked.

I shrugged and glanced at the digital clock on the television. I, too, was exhausted from worry. "It's 1:30 and we still haven't heard from him," I said.

For years I'd heard the phrase, *Let go and let God.* But I had worried for months about how to handle my son. Maybe it was time to turn my wandering son over to the Lord. But this time I knew I had to leave my child in God's hands—instead of taking him back.

I sat at the kitchen table, bowed my head, and prayed. In that moment I felt a complete peace wash over me as I turned my son over to the Lord.

"I have put him totally and completely in God's hands," I told my husband. I crawled into bed knowing God was in control. A short while later, I felt my husband slip into bed beside me.

At 2 A.M. the ringing phone jarred us awake. Sleepily, I answered. The police officer on the other end of the line informed me that once again my teenager was in jail. This time he had started a fight with a bouncer in a hotel lounge. When the security people found that he had a gun, seven or eight police cars arrived, screeching, on the scene. I was relieved to learn the gun was unloaded, but it didn't make the charges any less serious.

"I've been praying about this," my husband said after I hung up, "and I feel a real peace about what I'm about to say. I don't think we should bail him out of jail again."

A lump stuck in my throat, and I tried to swallow. I knew, after all the times my son had been jailed for drunk driving, that my husband was right. But it was hard to turn away from my own son. Yet I had to put my trust in God and my husband—we would not waver.

When my son called the next morning asking us to put up bail, my husband simply said, "We are through bailing you out of jail. This time you'll have to get out on your own." My husband sighed as he hung up. "He's mad," he said.

I often wondered how a parent could not come to a child's rescue. I had to learn the hard way that if I continued to shield my child from the consequences of his actions, he would never learn to take responsibility. And he would continue to get into trouble.

A few days later my son came home. He didn't speak to either of us except to say, "I'm moving out." He and a friend loaded his car with my son's belongings and left.

Several months went by before I heard from him again. Then one day he drove into the driveway with a blonde-haired girl at his side. He was smiling as he and the young lady came into the house, and the four of us sat down in the living room to talk. I was delighted to learn he wanted to get married, and although I had some well-founded apprehension about his anger problem, I certainly hoped he and his future wife would be happy.

As the days, weeks, and months flew by, I began to see a profound change in my married son. The angry young man who had left our home seemed to melt away as he worked to build his own family. And eventually, to my great joy, he turned his life over to God.

On one of our first Christmases together after his marriage, my son drove to the store with my husband. The cab of the truck was almost silent except for the radio playing softly. My son broke the quiet with an unexpected question. "Can you ever forgive me for the pain I put you through?" he asked.

My husband smiled and put his arm around him. "I've already forgiven you," he said.

I thank the Lord for bringing my wandering son home. And I thank my husband for having a forgiving spirit and also welcoming him home with compassion, just as the father of the biblical prodigal son did.

And, yes, my son still brings me flowers. That same Christmas, he brought a gorgeous poinsettia and set it on my kitchen table. And just like he did when he was little, he said, "These are for you, Mama."

# 𝒯 COULDN'T LET GO OF MY CHILDREN, SO THEY LET GO OF ME

## JOAN CLAYTON

*Love is patient and kind. Love is not jealous or boastful or proud or rude.*

*Love does not demand its own way. Love is not irritable,*

*and it keeps no record of when it has been wronged.*

1 CORINTHIANS 13:4-5 NLT

I suppose I thought it would last forever. What wonderful years we had. Rock hunting, picnics, Little League, band, basketball…and all the other fun things you do with your kids. Birthdays and holidays centered on our sons.

Of course we had our share of anxious moments. Trips to the hospital in the middle of the night for croup, and accidents in the daytime that required immediate attention.

One accident in particular is emblazoned on my memory. Our two younger boys were playing Blind Man's Bluff. Lane, the youngest, being blindfolded, stumbled over a jagged rock, fell, and hit his head. A big knot appeared on his forehead, and my husband, Emmitt, took him to the emergency room immediately. The wound wasn't serious, and so the attendants treated Lane and then sent them home.

When I returned home from shopping, I found Mark, our oldest son, in tears. Lance, our middle son, had apparently felt guilty about Lane's accident, and he had disappeared. Next to the door was a note:

*Dear Dad, I've run away. I cause too much trouble.*

*Bye. Lance*

We searched and searched. We drove up and down and all around, but no Lance appeared.

Finally the family dog sniffed Lance out; he was hiding behind the butane tank. Relief flooded my heart as Emmitt swooped Lance up in his arms and showered him with kisses.

Many mornings we awakened to find three lively boys in our bed. After the inevitable wrestling match, we would all end up in the floor in uncontrollable laughter.

When I caught them red-handed in the cookie jar, they tried to throw me off track. "Mommy, will you marry us when we grow up?"

I did not realize how quickly the years slipped by. Mark's wedding came all too quickly for us. The hardest part for me hit home when I went into his room and opened his closet. The shock of seeing the bare, empty shelves triggered an outburst of tears.

The closet was empty—except for one tiny bowl. It contained his two front teeth, a cat's-eye marble, two round pebbles for skipping on water, and a little rusty chain. I collapsed on the bed. *Is this all there is?* I pondered. *Where had the time gone?*

I struggled to let go, even though he was married. I expected our relationship to stay the same. I still looked at him as my little boy. Naturally we didn't see him as much, and in my self-pity, I interpreted this as rejection.

Everywhere I turned, I saw reminders of him. The white paint still lingered on the red brick wall where he and his brother had had a paint fight. The paint finally wore off the dog's fur, but it was still on the house to remind me.

I felt Mark had deserted his family…after everything we had done for him. I didn't realize that he desperately needed his independence, the freedom to make his own decisions and be the man of his own household. I went around with my feelings on my shoulder, bandaged in a giant dose of "poor little me."

By the time our middle son married, I had turned into a real clinging vine. I had caused him to be almost psychologically dependent on my husband and me. How I thank God he had an understanding wife who helped him mature, in spite of me. After his college graduation, they moved a thousand miles away. My heart ached until I thought it couldn't hurt anymore.

"I can't tell you good-bye!" I cried.

"But Mom," Lance replied, holding me with all the might of his 6'4" frame, "a Christian never has to say good-bye."

By this time, our youngest son, Lane, was graduating from high school. I told him, "Lane, when you walk across that stage, I'm going to run up there, grab you, and say, 'That's my baby!'"

Lane knew I wouldn't dare, but he did something that graduation night that is forever sealed in my heart.

Emmitt, being the high-school principal, always announced each graduate's name and then shook his or her hand. He had always treated our boys like any other student while they were at school, so he naturally was only going to shake Lane's hand.

But when he announced, "Tony Lane Clayton," amid the applause and cheers of the other students, Lane walked right up to his daddy, embraced him with outstretched arms, and held him close. I burst into tears.

A minister came to me after the graduation ceremony. "You must have a wonderful family. It is very rare to see a boy show such affection to his parents in public." I cried again.

Two years later, I cried some more. Lane cried too. He had packed his car with all his possessions, ready to leave home.

"But why are you leaving?" I cried.

"You have been great parents, but it's time for me to grow up."

By now Lane had discovered through his brothers' experiences that his independence could only be achieved away from me.

Looking back, I can see that in many ways my own emotional insecurity had forced my children to flee the nest. Unlike the eagle who pushes her babies out of the nest, I would have clung to them until the nest disintegrated.

It is still hard for me, even now with six grandchildren. It takes about a week to get over seeing them, wishing the time had not passed so quickly.

I have the same feeling every May when I tell my second graders good-bye at school. I think, *Why didn't I love them more and teach them less?*

The boys are happy leading their own lives and I'm thankful. Sure, they make mistakes. When they first started to walk, we didn't stop them, even though we knew they would fall sometimes. The same is true when they leave the nest. They are going to fall sometimes. How else can they learn? It goes against nature to try to keep them from developing. But by not letting them go, I was "stunting their growth." Can you think of a mother cat carrying her baby kitten around by the nape of the neck its entire life?

As a dear friend said to me one day, "In order to keep them, you have to let them go."

I have finally learned to put my children in God's hands and trust Him. He loves them even more than I do. My role has now changed from that of being a parent to being a strong supporter and friend.

Now I can see that the many years I gave to my kids were not in vain. Now I can say to the world: *Look out, here they come! They're going to make you better, happier, and sweeter. Why? They always knew they were loved!*

# ℳOTHER KNOWS BEST

## JENNIFER JOHNSON

*She speaks with wisdom, and faithful instruction is on her tongue.*

PROVERBS 31:26 NIV

Tears fell in solid lines down both cheeks. I threw open the front door of my parent's home and stomped inside.

"Mom!" My wail brought the thin, dark-haired woman into the living area. I kicked the door shut and threw my crumpled clothes onto the couch.

"Jennifer, what is it?"

"I'll never go back. I hate him."

"What's da matter, Jamfer?" Two-year-old Tabitha pulled on the hem of my shirt. My brothers, five-year-old Matthew and twelve-year-old Nick, shared the same worried expression as my baby sister.

I ignored them. Seventeen and already married, I had no need for whiny siblings.

I cried harder. Liquid drained from my eyes and nose. I ran

into the bathroom, flopped onto the toilet seat cover, and wiped my face with tissues. After several moments of deep breathing, I controlled my emotions and walked out of the room to search for my mother.

The smell of fried chicken assailed my senses. "She's in the kitchen," I mumbled to myself, and followed the scent. I sat at the kitchen table, clasped my hands, and twirled my thumbs round and round.

"Mom, I can't stand it. Albert is awful to live with. He's always grouchy. He's always mean. I hate him."

Mom didn't say a word.

"I don't want to be married to him anymore. Maybe we could get an annulment. Our marriage was a mistake."

A timer beeped. The food was ready. Mom dished up plates for my brothers and sister and then handed me an empty plate. I felt like one of the kids again. Puzzled by the feeling, I stood and dished out a little food for myself. Did I really want to be one of the kids again?

I thought of the freedom of my marriage. I could cook what I wanted, when I wanted. I could wear what I wanted, when I wanted. Did I really want to be in my mother's kitchen eating food she prepared as I had just one month before?

Albert's bullish face flooded my mind. The fight we'd had before he deposited me at my parent's house played afresh in my head.

"Get your things, Jennifer!" Albert's livid tone echoed through our small apartment. Fire lit his eyes as he opened the front door and pointed into the hallway leading to the outside of the building. "You are going home."

"That's fine!" I slung my purse over my shoulder and grabbed an armful of clothes. In a dead sprint, I raced past him and down the outside stairs. My destination, the single car we shared.

Without a driver's license, I was at his mercy. I slid into the passenger seat of the Mustang and waited. My body jumped at the slam of the apartment door. Within moments, Albert's tall, broad form appeared on the stairs. He opened the driver's side and fell into his seat. With angry movements, he started the car, threw the gear into reverse, and skidded out of the parking lot.

Tears welled in my eyes. I smacked them back with one hand. He would never have the pleasure of seeing my pain. "I hate you, Albert Johnson." The words snapped from my tongue. I meant them.

"Yeah, well, the feeling's mutual."

He dodged traffic, barely slowing for stop signs and racing through yellow caution lights. My hands trembled as I snapped my seatbelt across my waist. I prayed I'd make it to my destination alive. He pulled onto the gravel road to my parent's house and sped up the drive. The car skidded to a stop. He jumped out, raced around the car to the passenger side, and flung the door open. "Get out!"

Everything in me refused to allow this wretched being to see the hurt enveloping my soul. I stood to my full height and squared my shoulders against my husband. "You will not tell me what to do."

"You're right." He leaned over and grabbed the mass of clothes in the floorboard then thrust them into my hands. "I won't tell you what to do. I don't care what you do."

He ran around the car and jumped into the driver's seat. Without a second look, he was gone.

"Ouch." Mom's voice interrupted my thoughts. She kissed the tip of the finger she'd just burnt on the side of the skillet. She turned on the faucet in the sink and thrust her hand under the water.

The pain of Albert's rejection pierced my heart; the weight of sorrow slumped my shoulders. No, I couldn't go back to him. I would have to relinquish the freedom of married life for a while.

My mind replayed the evening Albert and I had shared our wedding vows. "I do." Two tiny words, three miniscule letters, but they had changed my life. Sure, it was hard to utter those words when one was a mere seventeen years old, but I had taken the plunge anyway.

Despite my anger, I couldn't stop my grin as I remembered

our first night in our apartment.

"Here we are." My new husband, arms filled with boxes, opened the door to our apartment located over an antique mall on Main Street.

I walked into the living room. Excitement coursed through my blood. This was my new home—mine and Albert's. With stars in my eyes, I envisioned delicious meals set before Albert on our dining-room table. I could see him slice generous portions of roast beef for both of us. We would share our days with each other, and laugh until our sides hurt. After our meal, Albert, so thankful and appreciative of my cooking abilities, would offer to help me with the dishes. At night I pictured us snuggled together on the sofa to enjoy a television program, or maybe just one another.

It didn't turn out that way.

I snapped from my reverie when my mother sat down at the table. She took a bite of food.

Nothing ever happened like I planned.

Frustration boiled within me. "I could take my maiden name back. I refuse to allow him to treat me this way. He's not worth it. I hate him." I spooned a bite of potatoes. No taste. I might as well have bit into air.

Soon my siblings placed their dishes in the sink. Mom took my partially empty plate from the table as well as hers. She plugged the sink, added soap to the running water, and then picked up her dishcloth and washed a plate.

"I'm young. I could find a different guy. One who would treat me right, and love me as I should be loved. Albert isn't worth it. He doesn't deserve me."

Mom finished the dishes and wiped the table and cabinets. She walked away. I followed her into the living room where she picked up my clothes and disappeared out the front door.

I stood motionless. She reappeared empty-handed.

"Mom, what are you doing?"

"Kids, get in the car," she motioned to the younger children. "You too," she pointed at me. "Get your purse."

"Mom?"

She trailed my siblings out the front door and into the station wagon. Dumbfounded, I followed.

"Mother, what are you doing?"

"Come on, Jennifer." She motioned for me to sit beside her in the station wagon.

With no other options, I got in.

"Where are we going?"

She didn't respond.

Slouched in the seat, I crossed my arms in front of my chest. Why wouldn't she talk to me? I was her daughter, for crying out loud. My husband had proven to be mean, grouchy, and difficult to live with. I didn't love him anymore. He didn't love me anymore.

Why wouldn't Mom talk to me?

Soon she turned onto a familiar street, and then pulled into a very familiar parking lot. I stared in disbelief at the staircase leading to Albert's and my apartment.

"What are you doing?" Panic rose in my throat threatening to strangle me. "Didn't you hear anything I said?"

Mom turned off the car and turned to face me. "Yes, I heard everything you said." Exhaustion etched her face. She rubbed her forehead. "You're young, but you made a commitment."

For a moment, she stared out her window. Her body shifted to face me again. She pointed toward the upstairs apartment. "Go up there and work this out."

Renewed anger flooded my soul. My mother was just as bad as my husband—no, worse. I was her own flesh and blood, yet she had chosen to throw me out. I felt like a sheep being thrown to the wolves, and by my very own mom.

"Fine," I squalled and jumped out of the car, grabbing only half the clothes I'd taken with me. I raced up the stairs and rapped on the door until my surprised husband opened it.

"What are you doing here?" Albert snapped.

I looked out the window. My mom's station wagon pulled out of the parking lot. I knew the scowl had not left my face as

I turned to face Albert.

"Don't start with me. Mom made me come home."

"Why?" The single word spit through his teeth in semi-controlled rage.

"She said we had to work this out."

And we did—more than twelve years ago.

# $\mathscr{P}$ICTURE OF A HOME

## JUDY BRIGGS

*Except the* LORD *build the house, they labour in vain that build it.*

PSALM 127:1

"A SMALL HOUSE WILL HOLD AS MUCH HAPPINESS AS A MANSION."

*Anonymous*

Tom and Judy decided that a life in the country would be a better place to raise their two young boys—Mike, who was eight, and Josh, who was five—rather than exposing them to the crime and pollution of the big city. They bought a small farm in rural Indiana, and despite their full-time jobs, they were determined to work the land themselves and make their farm a happy home for their family.

To call their farmhouse a fixer-upper would have been putting it kindly. The wind rattled through the cracked windowpanes and the creaks in the walls almost made Tom and Judy fear that the house might actually fall in on itself. Nonetheless, the fireplace was warm, the kitchen was cozy, and the kids had plenty of room to play outdoors.

In addition to their regular jobs, Tom and Judy found

themselves the new owners of half a dozen lambs and about twenty calves. To feed and water this new "zoo," as Judy came to call their menagerie, was backbreaking work. Hauling water and feed back and forth to the barn seemed easy enough at first, but soon the day-to-day grind became wearisome, and colder temperatures began to indicate that winter was fast approaching.

*Did I really pray for this?* Judy wondered at times. When she and Tom had prayed about their decision to make such a lifestyle change, they were certain that this was what God had wanted them to do. But now that day seemed so long ago.

The winter months arrived with a vengeance. The temperatures dipped so low that before they could haul the water to the barn, it would freeze. To make matters worse, Tom had to leave town for a few days in late February, leaving Judy to care for the farm and the boys on her own.

After a few days of lugging the water and feed through the snow, Judy had had about all she could take. She sat down wearily in her kitchen and looked out the window. *Please, God, give me a sign that this is where You want us to be.* When she looked up, she realized it was time to pick up the boys from school. She got into the truck and began to negotiate the icy roads into town, stopping on the way to pick up their mail at the local post office.

Inside the mailbox was a thick envelope that had been

postmarked back in Chicago, the city from where the family had moved. *It's from my best friend, Susan!* Judy was excited until she opened the letter and the photos of Susan's new home spilled out. *Look at that. It looks like something out of a magazine.* Judy's eyes filled with tears of frustration as she thought of her own ramshackle house back at the farm. Why couldn't God have given me that kind of life?

As the boys scrambled into the truck, they began to talk excitedly about their day at school. Josh especially couldn't wait to tell about his turn at show-and-tell. He had wanted to bring in one of the calves he had learned to feed, but Judy had convinced him that it would be better to take a photograph to school instead. It was this photo that Josh now held in his hands as his mother buckled him into his seat.

As Judy pulled onto the winding country road that led to their farm, she thought again of everything that Susan had that she herself had given up. Tears filled her eyes, and her vision blurred. Without warning, a blaring horn sounded, and Judy realized she had veered into the opposite lane. When she swerved to avoid the oncoming truck, the car began to skid on the ice. The last thing Judy saw was the tree approaching fast in the windshield. Then everything went black.

When she awoke, Judy was in a hospital room. Tom was leaning over her face, "Judy, are you awake? Talk to me, honey."

"What happened?" she asked groggily. And then she remembered. Panicking, she cried out, "Where are the boys? Are they okay?"

And then she saw them. Mike and Josh's faces were peering at her from the side of the bed, their expressions filled with worry. But when Judy smiled at them and weakly tousled Mike's hair, they both began to grin.

"Mom, my picture was the best in all of show-and-tell!" Josh reported proudly.

As Judy looked at the photograph, she realized God was giving her the sign she had asked for. Her child's face beamed into the camera, full of pride that he was hand-feeding his first calf. Judy began to understand that this was the picture God wanted for her life—a home filled with love, joy, and peace.

*Dear Lord, forgive me for not counting the blessings You have given me,* Judy prayed. *Thank You for bringing us here to this place, right where we belong.*

# MIRACLE IN THE RAIN

## JAN COLEMAN

*We know that God causes everything to work together for the good of those*

*who love God and are called according to his purpose for them.*

ROMANS 8:28 NLT

My daughter drove furiously up a mountain freeway in a rainstorm. Her vehicle hydroplaned and flipped upside down, along with my world as I knew it.

Carl and I inched our way to the hospital, driving through gushing steams of water. I was numbed by the news of Jennifer's accident. Carl was silent. We knew no details, only that Jennifer had been airlifted to a trauma center twenty miles away.

My heart cried out, *Please, Lord, don't let my daughter die with a wall between us.*

For the past year, Jen had been on a mad dash from her problems. With her marriage unraveling, her natural spunk turned every family gathering into a sparring match. Outwardly she seemed shockproof, in complete control, but inside Jennifer was still a fragile young girl with broken dreams, aching for the father who had abandoned his family years ago. I tried to mend the wounds in her life with a mother's counsel and correction, but my unwelcome words only made her more defensive.

She hadn't spoken to me in more than two months.

At the hospital, the neurosurgeon grimly said, "Surprisingly, she has only a few broken ribs, but she does have a serious head injury." She was in "bad shape." His dismayed look said it all. He didn't think she would make it.

So this is where the rubber meets the road when it comes to faith, Lord?

When we entered the hospital chapel, we found her husband, Steve. "We had a terrible fight last night, and I said some awful things." He spoke the words—his face filled with pain.

As I sobbed, Romans 8:28 came to mind: "All things work together for good...." How many times had I spouted that verse to someone in crisis? Did I really believe it now?

All things? Even tragic car accidents?

Then it hit me. Fretting would not change the outcome. Panicking would do no good. If I trusted God, as I claimed I did, I must cast all doubts aside. My daughter's life was in God's hands. My heart breaking, I told God, *I trust You, no matter what. I'll praise You, no matter what.* That was the toughest thing I ever promised to do.

Jen lay in a coma, her swollen, shaved head hooked to tubes, wires, and pressure monitors. Machines blipped and beeped while nurses worked frantically to keep her blood pressure stable. If not, death could steal her at any moment. And even if she did survive, brain damage was likely.

*God, give me Your perspective on this. My spiritual eyes are too blurry.* I looked up and saw Jenny, so peaceful, so beautiful. God seemed to be restoring her soul while she slept.

A voice pulled me from my thoughts. "How's my girl?" a young hospital technician asked.

"I was at the accident scene with this little lady," Phillip then told me.

He'd been heading down the mountain when he saw a massive crash ahead and a tiny dot catapult from the sun roof of a car; it was Jennifer, whose body crash-landed on the freeway just inches from her mangled vehicle.

"It took me three, four minutes to get there," Phillip explained. "I was late to work, but something told me I had to stop." He saw the highway patrol officer cover Jen's curled, lifeless body with a yellow slicker. Turning to call the coroner, the officer waved Phillip away. "She's not going to make it." But Phillip shot back, "I won't believe that!"

Trained as a Navy field medic, he went to work on my daughter. Finally, she gasped a breath. But it wouldn't be enough. Her only hope was in the rescue helicopter that hovered in the sky, unable to land because of the fierce rain and wind that battered the roadway. Just then another car pulled up, an off-duty EMT who had seen the commotion. He just happened to have a respirator in his car.

Minutes later, the storm quieted, and the helicopter landed.

I imagined an image of Jesus darting to catch Jennifer, His body cushioning her against a deadly fall that could have broken her body. I envisioned the Savior prompting Phillip to stop, directing the scene, clearing the raging skies for the circling helicopter.

Then I knew what it meant to have a peace that passes all understanding.

According to the doctor's charts, Jennifer's condition was not a hopeful one. It didn't matter. God works from His own heavenly charts.

Carl and I arrived for church early the next day to update our pastor on Jen's condition. God reached down and hugged us through the arms of the congregation. When I opened the bulletin I shook my head in disbelief: The title of the sermon was "God's Purpose for My Problems," the message being that how we respond to problems reveals what we believe about God.

All we could do was pray and wait. But I had a silent hopefulness that had no earthly explanation, and all my friends asked me, "Are you in shock?"

God was at work, and I was in awe of what He would do next.

A few days later my former husband, whom we hadn't seen in seven years, showed up at the hospital. Taking one look at his Jennifer on a breathing machine, he hung his head. "Can we talk somewhere?"

I sat facing the man who'd ripped my heart out, who'd turned his back on his young children.

"If I hadn't walked out on you," he said, "none of this would have happened. She's just like me, reckless and immature, running away from herself. I'm sorry I messed up our marriage, Jan. You were a good wife. None of this would be happening if I hadn't left you. Will you forgive me?"

How I'd dreamt of hearing those very words, but now thinking, *his concern comes awfully late.* I wanted to launch into a full report, make sure he knew all the details of the struggles we'd had because of his selfish choices, how his daughters were forever scarred, but those words wouldn't come out. All I could manage to utter was, "I forgave you long ago." and we wept together.

As God's grace poured over me, the last remnants of my own pain melted away

I couldn't sleep that night; my emotions shifted like a flag tossed in the wind. I'd wanted my daughters to be restored to their father, but now I was troubled by it. Jennifer was just beginning to bond with my husband, Carl. And now her biological dad, had come waltzing in, right in the middle of the crisis, sincere at the moment, but would he follow through and hurt her again?

As I laid anxious and awake, I felt the Lord tug at my heart, *Jan, I'm in control. Leave the results up to Me.*

The next day, Jen twitched a foot and began to emerge from the coma. The doctors shook their heads in amazement. Not only was she not paralyzed, she would recover. "A miracle," they said. Ten days later we transferred her to a rehabilitation hospital.

The doctors said they'd never seen such progress after a brain injury. Jen's fighting spirit played in her favor now, kicking in while she pushed to walk, formulate sentences, even chew her food again. The staff had never seen such amazing progress.

There was a refreshing softness to my daughter, one I hadn't seen since she was a child. One day as I sat by her bed and stroked her half-shaved curls, her words touched my heart: "Mom, I never want to fight with you again. I realize how much you love me and want the best for me. I want to learn how to be a better wife and grow closer to God."

Three months after the accident, Jennifer walked shakily into her own house, back to Steve and two young sons. And now, five years later, she's made almost a full recovery from a severe brain injury.

I look at my daughter differently now. While Jen's strength and determination were a past source of conflict for me, I now see they are actually gifts from God, and He intends to use them to do great things in her life. My daughter is a precious stone in the Master's hand that He is crafting for His glory. And He doesn't need my help. I've given up my advice-giving. I've stopped trying to fix her. I seek God's perspective first. That's the way to find the purpose in our problems.

People in our small town still talk about "the miracle in the rain," the rescue, the amazing recovery.

But to me there is still yet another miracle—having my daughter as my friend.

# *C*OURAGE

GLORIA CASSITY STARGEL

*I will love thee, O LORD, my strength.*

PSALM 18:1

The call came in the middle of a scorching Saturday afternoon. Our younger son Rick, stationed at Cherry Point Marine Corps Air Station in North Carolina, had been admitted to the hospital with a ruptured appendix. "They brought him down to Camp Lejeune and performed surgery," his friend reported, " but I can't find him."

Fear took over as I suspected the worse. A ruptured appendix can be fatal. "We'll be there as soon as we can," I said, but we were two entire states away. *Oh, God, please help Rick.*

I called Joe in from mowing the lawn and, frantic, he phoned Camp Lejeune, locating the surgeon. "Yes, I operated on your son this morning," he said. "The infection had spread into the surrounding tissues. We're leaving the incision open in case we have to go back in." That means peritonitis has set in.

*Lord, help.* My courage began to vanished.

"I have to tell you," the doctor added, "he is a very sick boy. But he's young, and he's in good physical shape. I think he'll make it." *Oh, Lord, give us all courage and strength.*

Joe never talks while driving, so I had practically all night to think—and worry.

Why in the world did Rick wait so long before seeing a doctor? Then my wandering mind reasoned, *Why am I surprised?* The Marine Corps evidently teaches its men they can withstand anything—that they're invincible.

I should know. Joe himself is a Marine to the core. Semper Fidelis—always faithful. He enlisted at age seventeen and now, with the rank of Major, served with a reserve unit in Atlanta. The fact that Rick followed in his dad's footsteps shouldn't have surprised me.

On the open road this night, the steady drone of the car engine provided the only sound. Soon we were swallowed up in blackness, blackness relieved only by the streetlights of an occasional sleeping town.

Continuing my reverie, I contemplated the crucial factor that had influenced Rick, affected us all, for that matter. Four years earlier we had faced another surgical crisis when Joe was diagnosed with incurable cancer. Although he appeared to be beating the odds, the outcome as yet was uncertain. It had been particularly demoralizing for him when the Marine Corps declared him medically unable to serve. Just recently, though, he had been reinstated to active status and even dared to hope for a promotion in rank.

This specter of uncertainty about his dad's health had clouded the years Rick was in college. The week he received his degree, he cut his hair short, shaved off his beard, and joined the Corps. "Somebody's got to carry on the tradition," he explained.

I recall vividly the heart-wrenching day he flew off for basic training at Officer Candidate School. After all, just twenty years earlier he was my little bundle of joy. Most mothers will tell you—we never fully give up feeling they're our babies. *Lord, help me once again to keep the faith in a crisis, to trust You in all things—even this.*

At 3 A.M. in the morning we reached the Camp Lejeune hospital, a soon-to-be-replaced red brick building, three stories tall, dark now except for a smattering of dim lights on each floor.

Inside, our footsteps echoed down dismal hallways. A squeaky elevator emptied us onto the third floor where at the far end, a small lamp revealed a desk and the silhouette of a nurse bent over her paperwork. We approached her and asked about our son. She looked up, gave us the once-over, and said, ever so kindly, "Would you like to see him?"

"Oh, yes! May we?"

"Follow me," she said. With that, she picked up a flashlight, flicked it on, and cut us a path down the black asphalt-tiled floor of yet another gloomy corridor.

"He's in the room with another patient," the nurse said softly, motioning us through a door. "We'll need to be as quiet as possible."

We barely could detect Rick's bed in the shadows. Following the sounds of muted groans, being careful of the IV-dispensing contraption with its tubes and bottles, I touched his shoulder. His hospital gown was drenched with perspiration. "Rick," I whispered, bending close to his ear, "it's Mother and Dad."

Our very groggy son answered, "I'm glad you're here."

I leaned over and kissed his fevered brow, "I love you."

"'Love you, too," he managed. Then drifted back into a medicine-induced sleep.

*Lord, our boy here needs Your healing touch. And, Lord, about that courage—I need it now, real bad.*

Rick was alert the next day—Sunday—but still feverish and miserable with pain.

On Monday morning, Joe let me out at the front door to the hospital while he found a parking space. The hallways, quiet all weekend, now bustled with activity. White-uniformed nurses and corpsmen hurried in and out of rooms; patients—all wearing U.S. Navy-issued blue cotton robes and scuffs—shuffled through the halls.

When I reached Rick's room, he lay flat on his back, anxiously eyeing the door. "Where's Dad?" he asked hurriedly, a note of excitement in his voice.

"He's parking the car."

"Can you help me get up?" he said, painfully pushing the sheet back with his feet and with great effort raising himself on one elbow, "I've got to be standing when Dad gets here."

I sensed this was no time for questions. Taking his arms while he clenched his teeth against the pain, I pulled him around into a sitting position on the edge of the bed, then sat down beside him. While he held his incision with one hand, he placed his other arm around my shoulder. I, in turn, put one arm around his back with my other hand steadying his IV pole, and somehow we stood to the floor. We propped the back of his legs against the bed for support. Then he motioned me to ease away.

Just in time. Masculine footsteps in the hall.

Joe barely got inside the room when he stopped in his tracks, not believing what he saw: Rick, standing by his bed. Then Rick pulled himself to almost-full height, snapped to attention, and with a crisp salute heralded, "Congratulations,

Colonel, Sir!"

"Wha—wha—what???" Joe stammered, totally bewildered.

"Your promotion came through!" Rick reported, a big grin forming. "Colonel Asher called this morning from Atlanta. You're a Lieutenant Colonel!"

"Promotion? Called here? How did he find me here?"

To describe Joe as dumbfounded would be a gross understatement. He was undone! Oh, but for a video camera to record the event. Suddenly, it all sank in and his face lit up like the Fourth of July!

And just as suddenly, the Marine in him sprang back to life. With his officer demeanor engaged, he "snapped to," and— even though he was wearing civilian clothes which ruled out an official salute—returned Rick a quick, informal one. "Thank you, Lieutenant."

Then with two long strides Joe reached Rick and enfolded him in a giant bear hug. I joined in to make it a threesome. We laughed and cried, all at the same time, realizing that probably no promotion had ever come at a more tender moment.

After we helped Rick back into bed, he furnished a perfect finish to the stirring scene. Reverting to his affectionate title for his dad, he said, "We're awfully proud of you, Pa."

Pa, the new Colonel. We were "just family" once again.

Yet, I dare say, a changed family. For etched forever in my

heart is the picture of that young feverish Marine in a wrinkled, bobtailed hospital gown, barely able to stand, snapping to attention and honoring his dad! What a memorable moment! What courage! Semper Fi—to the core!

I borrowed some of that courage the next day when Joe and I left for home. Our tear-mingled embraces followed three lump-throated good-byes.

Yet, as we drove away, I felt at peace, confident that our boy would get well. For the surgeon had pointed out that Rick was young and strong physically. Now, with that memorable moment, God had allowed me to see evidence of his inner strength as well. My faith was secure once again. God was looking after our son. And me.

# ROCK MUSIC, ROCKY, AND RACHMANINOFF

## SUSAN JENNINGS

*Make a joyful noise to the LORD!*

PSALM 98:4

One Saturday morning when the phone rang, I rushed past my son's bedroom to answer it. *Lucky I even heard it,* I thought. Sixteen-year-old Tony had taken up the electric guitar and drums, and his hard rock music sometimes drowned any other conversation, or sound, for that matter. For months his dad and I had argued with Tony about his music, and I was reaching the end of my rope. I couldn't stand the racket, I couldn't stand the lyrics, and I was worried about the influence that kind of music might have on my son. My constant prayer was a cry to the Lord for peace and quiet!

But the phone call I received brought another crisis: It was my friend Kathleen, who was preparing to move to England. "I just found out that I can't take Rocky with me," she said.

Rocky, her gray tabby cat of eight years, meant the world to Kathleen. "If I can't find a home for her, I don't know what I'll do! Would you consider taking her in?"

Without warning, a yellow flash zipped across the countertop and landed in the butter dish. Our new kitten, Missy, had struck again. "Get out of there!" I yelled. Then Princess, our German shepherd, sauntered into the kitchen and cocked her head at me as if she understood my dilemma. I already had two pets. Could I handle a third? Kathleen waited for my response. "I'll think about it," I told her, hanging up the phone and surveying the butter tracks on the kitchen floor. At that moment Tony's music started upstairs again. My teeth clenched. It would be impossible to add another element to this circus.

And yet the idea nagged at me. When I broached the idea of yet another cat sharing our space, my husband and son said they wouldn't mind—it was up to me. I was going through my mental list of all the reasons not to take Rocky when I whispered a prayer *"Dear God, what should I do?"* I prayed. Something in my heart told me to say yes.

I called Kathleen with the good news. "Oh, thank you so much, Nancy. I know you two will be fast friends," she said. Then she reeled off Rocky's quirks: "She loves broccoli and classical music and—"

"Classical music?" I cut her off. Maybe this was God's idea

after all!

"Yes, believe it or not," Kathleen said. "It calms her. She purrs when it's playing."

On the day of Kathleen's departure, Tony and I went to pick up Rocky. Kathleen tearfully hugged her cat good-bye, then gave a last-minute admonition to my son: "Don't forget the classical music!"

On her arrival at our house, Missy and Princess sniffed the cat carrier and started hissing and barking. "Hey, Mom, Rocky can stay with me," Tony said. Before I could stop him, he hurried upstairs, carrying Rocky to her "safe" environment. Left to calm our pets downstairs, I didn't have the energy to intervene. I shuddered thinking of my son's room, complete with drums, electric guitars, and amplifiers. I just didn't see how this could end without more chaos.

The next morning Tony rushed off to school after a brief announcement that the night had gone well for Rocky. "Don't let her out of my room, Mom," he warned. "I have it all set up for her."

Of course I had to open his door a crack to check for myself. I couldn't believe my ears. Strains of Bach floated out to greet me. An obviously contented Rocky was perched next to the radio, purring away. My son, the rock fan, had set his radio to a classical station! I didn't realize Tony even knew such music existed.

Evenings passed with Tony doing math homework to the strains of Rachmaninoff. Mornings began not with electric guitars but with violins. As the days passed, rock selections still emitted from the room from time to time, but more and more there were concertos, sonatas, and symphonies.

The other animals settled down, and as I did my morning chores we all enjoyed the sound of Haydn drifting from Tony's room.

God had answered my prayer by bringing harmony to the whole household. But He did it in a most unusual way: He had sent Rocky, the cat who craved classical music. I am proud to say that my son, after enjoying a brief stint playing in an alternative rock band, eventually chose a calmer form of music to focus on—he now plays classical guitar, and even plans to record some songs he has written in that genre. All because I took in a cat named Rocky. Or to be more precise, let go of my way of handling a situation that was rapidly spiraling out of control, and instead followed God's way.

# THE LITTLE RED WAGON

## PATRICIA LORENZ

*He orders his angels to protect you wherever you go.*

*They will steady you with their hands to keep you from*

*stumbling against the rocks on the trail.*

PSALMS 91:11-12. TLB

To be perfectly honest, the first month was blissful. When Jeanne, age six, Julia, four, and Michael, three, and I moved from Missouri to my hometown in northern Illinois the very day of my divorce from their father, I was just happy to find a place where there was no fighting or abuse.

But after the first month I started missing my old friends and neighbors. I missed our lovely, modern, ranch-style brick home in the suburbs of St. Louis, especially after we'd settled into the ninety-eight-year-old white frame house we'd rented, all my "post-divorce" income could afford.

In St. Louis we'd had all the comforts: a washer, dryer, dishwasher, TV, and a car. Now we had none of these. After the first month in our new home, it seemed that we'd gone from middle-class comfort to poverty-level panic.

The bedrooms upstairs in our ancient frame house weren't even heated, but somehow the children didn't seem to notice. The linoleum floors, cold on their little feet, simply encouraged them to dress faster in the mornings and hop into bed quicker in the evenings.

I complained about the cold as the December wind whistled under every window and door in that old frame house. But they giggled about the "funny air places" and simply snuggled under the heavy quilts Aunt Bernadine brought over the day we moved in.

I was frantic without a TV. "What will we do in the evenings without our favorite shows?" I asked. I felt cheated that the children would miss out on all the Christmas specials. But the children were more optimistic and much more creative than I. They pulled out their games and begged me to play "Candyland" and "Old Maid" with them.

We cuddled together on the gray tattered couch the landlord provided and read picture book after picture book from the public library. At their insistence we played records, sang songs, popped popcorn, created magnificent Tinker-Toy towers, and played hide-and-go-seek. The children taught me how to have fun without a TV.

One shivering December day, just a week before Christmas, after walking the two miles home from my temporary part-time job at a catalog store, I remembered that the week's laundry had to be done that evening.

I was dead tired from lifting and sorting other people's Christmas presents, and I was feeling somewhat bitter, knowing that I could barely afford any gifts for my own children.

As soon as I picked up the children at the babysitter's, I piled four large laundry baskets full of dirty clothes into the children's little red wagon, and the four of us headed toward the laundromat three blocks away.

Inside we had to wait for washing machines and then for people to vacate the folding tables. The sorting, washing, drying, and folding took longer than usual.

Jeanne asked, "Did you bring any raisins or crackers, Mommy?"

"No," I snapped. "We'll have supper as soon as we get home."

Michael's nose was pressed against the steamy glass window. "Look Mommy! It's snowing! Big flakes!"

Julia added, "The street's all wet. It's snowing in the air but not on the ground!"

Their excitement only upset me more. As if the cold weren't bad enough, now we had snow and slush to contend with. I hadn't even unpacked the box that held their boots and mittens yet.

At last the clean, folded laundry was stacked into the laundry baskets and placed two-baskets-deep in the little red wagon. It was pitch dark outside. Was it six-thirty already? No wonder they were hungry! We usually ate at five.

The children and I inched our way into the cold winter evening and slipped along the slushy sidewalk. Our procession of three little people, a crabby mother, and four baskets of fresh laundry in a red wagon moved slowly along as the frigid wind bit into our faces. We crossed the busy four-lane street at the crosswalk. When we reached the curb, the front wagon wheels slipped on the ice and tipped the wagon over on its side, spilling all the laundry into a slushy black puddle.

"Oh no!" I wailed. "Grab the baskets, Jeanne! Julia, hold the wagon! Get back up on the sidewalk, Michael!"

I slammed the dirty, wet clothes back into the baskets.

"I hate this!" I screamed. Angry tears spilled out of my eyes.

I hated being poor with no car and no washer or dryer. I hated the weather. I hated being the only parent responsible for three small children. And if the truth were told, I hated the whole blasted Christmas season.

When we reached home, I unlocked the door, threw my purse across the room, and stomped off to my bedroom for a good cry.

I sobbed loud enough for the children to hear. Selfishly I

wanted them to know how miserable I was. Life couldn't get any worse. The laundry was still dirty, we were all hungry and tired, there was no supper started and no outlook for a brighter future.

When the tears finally stopped, I sat up and stared at a wooden plaque of Jesus that was hanging on the wall at the foot of my bed. I'd had that plaque since I was a small child and carried it with me to every house I'd ever lived in. It showed Jesus with His arms outstretched over the earth, obviously solving the problems of the world.

I kept looking at His face, expecting a miracle. I looked and waited, and finally said aloud, "God, can't You do something to make my life better?" I desperately wanted an angel on a cloud to come down and rescue me.

But nobody came...except Julia, who peeked into my bedroom and told me in her tiniest four-year-old voice that she had set the table for supper.

I could hear six-year-old Jeanne in the living room sorting the laundry into two piles: "really dirty, sorta clean, really dirty, sorta clean...."

Three-year-old Michael popped into my room and gave me a picture of the first snow that he had just colored.

And at that very moment I did see, not one, but three angels before me! Three little cherubs, eternally optimistic and once again pulling me from gloom and doom into the world of "things will be better tomorrow, Mommy."

Christmas that year was magical as we surrounded ourselves with a very special kind of love, based on the joy of doing simple things together. One thing's for sure: single parenthood was never again as frightening or as depressing for me as it was the night the laundry fell out of the little red wagon. Those three angels have kept my spirits buoyed and today, more than twenty-five years later, they continue to fill my heart with the presence of God.

# $\mathcal{I}$T WAS A GOD THING

## TERESA GRIGGS

*"Since my youth, O God, you have taught me,*

*and to this day I declare your marvelous deeds."*

PSALM 71:17 NIV

"Wow, Mom, you should have seen the drive I hit on hole number eleven!" my son, Ryan, exclaimed as he met me on the cart path coming in from the eighteenth hole. "It was a God thing!"

He continued his story: "As I approached the tee box, I said a little prayer asking God to help me have a long drive. This was a long par five, and I needed a long drive that would stay in-bounds. So I took out my driver, and you know how I have been having some control problems with my driver…."

Sweat was pouring off his face, his heavy golf bag was still on his shoulders, and I wanted to suggest he set it down, but knew better than to interrupt his story. His face held a grin as he talked that made me smile as I listened.

"Oh, Mom, you should have been there!  I hit the ball and

immediately thought, *Oh, no!* The ball hooked over to the left, and I just knew it was headed out of bounds. Then the most amazing thing happened. It bounced off the concrete cart path."

He made the motion with his arm of the ball bouncing down and then way up high again.

"Then it went on down further and bounced on the path again and rolled just as pretty as you please right out in the middle of the fairway. Why, it was probably 450 yards down the fairway when it stopped rolling. It was simply a God thing!"

Ryan and I were in Kansas City, about eight hours from our hometown of Sikeston, Missouri for the Missouri Junior Amateur Golf Championship. He had been playing junior golf for several years. He and I enjoyed traveling during the summer months as he played in various tournaments. The time together was a blessing from the Lord. We discussed many things on those trips—his education, his future, his hopes and dreams, the truths of God's Word, and especially God's call on his life.

My husband, Darryl, and I have tried to give all of our children a firm foundation in God's Word and a Christian heritage of faith, but I have often wondered about their personal faith. Were they developing a personal and complete faith in God not only as their Savior, but also as their Friend? Do they know that God is there for them anytime, anywhere they call on Him?

As Ryan slept in the car on our way home that day, I thought about the times in my life when I too knew it was a God thing. I thought about the time in the sixth grade when I wanted to go to band camp—one full week of staying in the college dorms, practicing with students from all over the area. I was so excited as I went home with the registration form that evening. "It's only forty dollars for the whole week," I pleaded with my mother. "And everybody will be going."

"Well, let me talk to Dad about it," was her only reply.

When my Dad got home that evening for supper, I was too excited to wait until the right moment to ask. Being a wife and mother, I know now that you never ask Dad anything as soon as he walks in the door. But I was twelve years old, and I couldn't hold it in that long. I burst out, "Dad, band camp is this summer. It is only forty dollars to go. All my friends are going. Could I please, please go?"

My father was a good provider for our family. We always had everything we needed, but forty dollars would probably have paid for groceries for a week. His answer was an adamant "No!"

Once Dad made up his mind that was the end of it. He left after supper and was not at the house the rest of the night, so I could not have pleaded my case any further even if I thought it would have done any good.

As I went to bed, I talked with the Lord earnestly. Actually I begged God, *Please make Daddy change his mind and let me go!*

The next morning while Mom and I were in the kitchen, Dad walked in and announced, "Sis, if this band thing is so important, give Mom the form and we'll work it out."

That day things began to change in my twelve-year-old mind and spirit. I began to learn that the things that mattered to me, mattered to God. That God really cared for me and if I would trust in Him and follow His will, He would bless me with the desires of my heart. My faith began to grow.

Since that day, God has answered my prayers many times. Sometimes He has answered with a definite, *No.* But my faith in Him has continued to grow and mature, and I have never doubted that I could go to Him with anything, any decision, any problem or trial in my life.

Were my children learning that same faith? Were they learning that same trust in an all-knowing, all-loving heavenly Father? As Ryan shared with me how God had answered his prayer on the golf course that day, I realized that just as God used the ordinary, simple things to teach me faith in Him, He is also teaching my son.

# THE HUMBUG HOLIDAYS AND THE LEAN-TO SNOWMAN

## PATRICIA LORENZ

*We depend upon the LORD alone to save us.*
*Only he can help us; protecting us like a shield.*

PSALM 33:20 NLT

I was going through the motions—everything a good mom is supposed to do before Christmas. I lugged out the boxes of holiday decorations. Baked my every-year-the-same-two-kinds of cookies. And even bought a real Christmas tree for a change.

I was going through the motions, but my heart was bogged down with a dull ache. I wasn't looking forward to Christmas one bit. My divorce had been finalized the past April, and my ex-husband was already remarried.

My oldest daughter, Jeanne, was in Yugoslavia for the year as a foreign exchange student and wouldn't be home for the holidays. This was the first time that all four of my children wouldn't be with me for Christmas. Plus, the annual New Year's Eve get-together at my folks' house in Illinois had been canceled.

I was tired and grumpy. My job writing radio commercials at Milwaukee's biggest radio station became more hectic every day. Nearly every business in town wanted to advertise during the holiday season, and that meant longer and longer hours at work.

Then there was the real nemesis, holiday shopping, a chore I kept putting off. I was supposed to be planning and buying not only for my annual holiday party for the neighbors, but Andrew's eighth birthday on December 27, and Julia's seventeenth birthday on January 4 as well. How would I get through it all when "bah humbug" was on the tip of my tongue?

During the night of December 15, a snowstorm ripped through Wisconsin, dumping twelve inches of snow. Although Milwaukee is usually prepared for the worst, this blizzard finished its onslaught just before rush hour traffic, bringing the interstate highways to a standstill. The next day all the schools and most businesses were closed. Even the radio station where I worked, eighteen miles from my home, urged early-morning risers to stay in bed because the roads were impassable.

After viewing the picture-postcard scene outdoors, I forgot my down-in-the-dumps attitude, grabbed Andrew and said, "Come on, buddy, let's make a snowman!"

Andrew and I scooped up big handfuls of the wet, perfect-packing snow and built a base fit for a kingpin. Andrew rolled a ball of snow for the next level into such a huge mass that I had to get down on my hands and knees to shove it toward our mighty base.

When I hoisted Andrew's third boulder onto this Amazon snowperson, I felt like Wonder Woman pressing a hundred pounds. As our snowman reached a solid seven feet tall, I carefully placed Andrew's bowling-ball-sized snow head on top with the help of a stool.

"He needs a face, Mom." While I smoothed the snow and pounded arms and a waistline into our giant snowman, Andrew ran inside and returned with a silly beach hat with built-in sunglasses for eyes and a Superman cape that we plastered on the back of the giant.

Andrew and I stepped back to admire our noble snowman. Straight and tall. Ruler of the yard. When I took their picture, Andrew's head barely reached the snowman's middle.

It was warmer the next morning, and when I looked outside the kitchen window I noticed that Super Snowman seemed to lean forward a little. I hoped he wouldn't fall over before Andrew got home from school that day.

Late that afternoon when I returned home after a hectic, make-up-all-the-work-from-yesterday, day at the radio station,

I saw that our snowman hadn't fallen over, but leaned even farther forward at a very precarious forty-five-degree angle. His posture reminded me of the way I felt. Tired, crabby, out-of-sorts, and with the weight of the world on my shoulders.

The next morning Super Snowman continued so far forward that it almost seemed a physical impossibility. I had to walk out into the yard to see him up close. *What on earth is holding him up?* I wondered, absolutely amazed.

The Superman cape, instead of being around his neck, now dangled freely in the wind as old Frosty's bent chest, shoulders, and head were almost parallel to the ground.

My own shoulders sagged beneath the weight of depression each time I remembered that Christmas was almost here. A letter from Jeanne arrived saying that since Christmas wasn't a national holiday in Yugoslavia, she'd have to go to school on December 25. I missed Jeanne's smile, her wacky sense of humor, and her contagious holiday spirit.

The fourth day after we built the snowman was Saturday the nineteenth, the day I'd promised to take Andrew to Chicago on the train.

Andrew loved the adventure of his first train and taxi rides, the trip to the top of the world's tallest building, the visit to the Shedd Aquarium, and the toy departments of every major store on State Street. But I was depressed by the fact that it rained all day, that the visibility at the top of the Sears Tower was zero, and that the all-day adventure left me totally exhausted.

Late that night, after the two-hour train ride back to Milwaukee, Andrew and I arrived home, only to be greeted by the snowman, who by this time, after a warmer day of drizzling rain, was now totally bent over from its base and perfectly parallel to the ground...and yet still balanced six inches above the slushy snow.

*That's me out there,* I said to myself. *About to fall face down into a snowbank.* But why didn't our snowman fall? Nothing, absolutely nothing, supported the weight of that seven-foot-tall giant.

*Just like there isn't anything or anybody supporting me during this awful holiday season,* I blubbered mentally.

I wondered, *what had supported the snowman in such a precarious position? Was it God in His almighty power? A freak of nature? A combination of ice, wind, rain, and snow that had bonded to the mighty Super Snowman?* I had a feeling there was a lesson to be learned from watching his decline. The lesson came to me gradually during the next two weeks.

On Christmas Eve, at the children's insistence, we attended the family services at our parish church and dined on our traditional oyster stew afterwards. Then Andrew brought out the Bible for the yearly reading of the Christmas story before the children and I opened gifts.

Later we attended a midnight candle service with friends at their church and finally a phone call from Jeanne in Yugoslavia brimmed with good news of an impromptu Christmas celebration planned by the mother of the family she was staying with.

The next day some friends offered to co-host my big neighborhood party which turned into a smashing success. On December 27, Andrew was delighted with his three-person birthday party. The next weekend my out-of-town family got together for a long New Year's Eve weekend at my house, filling our home with the madcap merriment of ten houseguests who all pitched in to help with everything. And when Julia simplified another dilemma by saying that all she wanted for her birthday was a watch and "lunch out with Mom," I smiled all day.

I learned that no matter how depressed, overwhelmed, saddened, lonely, or stressed out we become, there's always someone or something to help us find or recapture our own inner strength, just like there was for the falling-down, stoop-shouldered Super Snowman.

During his four-day lifespan, he showed me an amazing strength from within…a strength that came to me gradually, bit by bit, as each person in my life stepped up to boost my faith and my spirits to heavenly skies.

It was indeed a holiday season to cherish.

# $\mathcal{O}$UT OF THE DARKNESS

## TONNA CANFIELD

*I will give you the treasures of darkness, riches stored in secret places.*

ISAIAH 45:3 NIV

It has been nearly two years since my descent into the world of depression. I'm not sure how long the depression had been going on before I actually acknowledged it—too long, that much I know. There are many words to describe all the things I was (or wasn't) feeling, but the word that describes it best is a very simple one: sad. I felt this terrible, overwhelming sadness. And I felt many things besides: anxious, isolated, and hopeless. I could find no joy or peace in anything.

I usually love to cook for my family, and I love to eat even more than I love to cook! But during that time I had no desire to eat, much less cook. I lost over twenty-five pounds in a very short period of time.

I usually love to sleep. I think that crawling under a warm blanket with a fluffy pillow and snuggling down for a nap is right up there among life's greatest pleasures. But during this time I was unable to sleep. I'm not talking about not sleeping well or tossing and turning during the night. I mean not sleeping. I watched the clock all night long, hour after hour after hour, longing for a good night's sleep, but it eluded me.

I had always absolutely loved doing things with my children. I couldn't even find joy in that anymore. My joy was gone. My peace was gone. Depression was no longer a word that I was vaguely familiar with, a word I had heard about, or a word I had even used carelessly from time to time when things weren't going well.

No, depression wasn't a stranger anymore or even a casual acquaintance. Depression had now become my closest companion. It was there with me day and night, alone and in a crowd, like a stalker that wouldn't go away. It was there at every moment, every occasion; not merely lurking around the corner, but dwelling within me at all times.

Much to my dismay, depression had become something I knew more about than I ever wanted to know. But worse than the constant presence of depression, the anxiety, the overwhelming sadness, the loss of friendships, and the isolation I felt from everyone else in the world, was the separation I felt from God. We are made to commune with God. There is a longing deep in every human being that only God can fill, and

I felt separated from Him. That was truly the worst agony of all. I was in such a pit of depression that I couldn't see God. I knew that the Bible says that He never leaves us or forsakes us but I couldn't see or feel Him in my darkness and it seemed that He had left, which brings me to something very important that I learned from being in that agonizing depression: Even though I could not see God in the darkness, He never lost sight of me. His eyes were on me the entire time.

Even still, He kept me safe in the darkness when I didn't feel safe. I could not see in the pitch black. God's vision was perfect, even in the darkness. His eyes never left me. I was not alone. There was One walking in the darkness with me. There was an unseen hand guiding me toward precious treasures.

One of the most valuable treasures God gave me was a prayer partner. I told a friend that I had gone to the doctor for depression. A few weeks later, she called and shared with me that she had been battling depression for several months and after our conversation had decided to seek medical treatment. That was the first time in months that I felt a hopeful connection to another person. I understood every emotion and lack of emotion that she described. I knew she truly understood how I felt. It was then that healing began to take place. We decided that day to start getting together several times a week to pray. In the beginning, we just sat on the couch and joined hands and asked God to help us. It has been nearly a year and half since we started praying together, and we still meet, join hands, and pray. We are now able to bear one another's burdens, lifting up prayers, not only for each other, but also for our husbands, children, families, and others.

My friend and I are both glad we sought medical treatment as well as each other's support. But more significantly, my journey through the darkness has taught me to trust God more. I don't feel like I have to see what lies ahead, and I'm confident that God is with me even during the times when I may not feel Him or see Him in the circumstances.

I have even noticed a change in the way I pray. I now realize that much of my prayer time was spent trying to persuade God to do what I wanted. I now find my prayers becoming more and more about submitting to God's way. There is a wonderful peace and freedom in submitting to His guidance. He is teaching me to love Him for who He is instead of for what He does for me. I came out of that bleak season with a stronger faith, a more submissive heart, a faithful friend and prayer partner, and a deep empathy for the millions who suffer from depression.

What a wonderful peace and hope inhabits my heart. How safe and reassuring to know God is there, close and watchful of every step I take.

# APPLE PIECES OF RESTORED LOVE

## KATHY COLLARD MILLER

*…Get rid of all bitterness, rage and anger…along with every*
*form of malice. Be kind and compassionate to one another,*
*forgiving each other, just as in Christ God forgave you."*

EPHESIANS 4:31-32, NIV

"BITTERNESS
IMPRISONS
LIFE; LOVE
RELEASES IT."

*Harry Emerson*
*Fosdick*

When Larry and I had been married for seven years, we
were completely disillusioned with each other. I couldn't
understand why Larry didn't love me anymore. He certainly
was far from being the Prince Charming I'd married. *Oh Lord,*
*what's wrong with him?* I moaned. *What's wrong with me? I*
*thought we were going to have a perfect marriage because You*
*brought us together. But now we're such strangers.*

I'd tried everything to restore the intimacy between us, but
nothing seemed to work. The very character qualities which
had attracted me to Larry when we were dating were now the
sources of irritation in our relationship. Why did I ever think

his ambitiousness and opinionated attitudes were charming?

One morning Larry announced he was flying to San Jose for the day. I quickly suggested, "I'll get the kids ready and we'll go with you..."

Larry interrupted me. "Kathy, I'm sorry, but you can't go. I rented a two-seater plane and I've already asked Joe to go with me."

"But Larry, we never see you. Can't you stay home just this once? You're either flying or working so many hours."

"Now, Kathy, I've already explained that I'm working all those hours to secure our financial future. You just don't appreciate all I'm doing for this family."

My face grew hot with fury. "Money isn't helping me cope with these kids!" I snapped. "Darcy makes me so angry sometimes."

"Kathy, that's just typical motherhood blues. You'll be fine. I've got to go now."

Larry walked away down the hall as I stood with my hands on my hips, trying to show my disapproval with a disgusted look on my face. I felt like screaming, "Why don't you love me anymore?"

He walked through the laundry room into the garage, closing the door behind him. To me it was as if he'd slammed it in my face. I had been eating an apple as our conversation started and before I realized it, my hand with the half-eaten apple pulled back behind my ear and sent it flying toward that door. The apple shattered on impact and red and white apple pieces flew throughout the laundry room adhering to the ceiling and the walls. I whirled around and marched into my bedroom, dropping to kneel beside my bed, I prayed the unthinkable, *Lord, make that plane crash! I don't care if he ever comes home again.*

Larry's plane didn't crash, but I felt as if my life had crashed...crashed into a pit of uncontrollable anger and depression. *If only I can make him see how much he's hurting me,* I thought. *If only I can make him stay home more...if only I can force him to do what I want him to do...then I will be happy.*

My angry efforts at manipulation, nagging, and control totally failed. During the following months, the pieces of apple remained adhered to the walls and ceiling of my laundry room and then began rotting. I saw them as a memorial to the rotten marriage I believed God could not or would not change.

One day several months later, I sensed God speak to my heart, *Tell Larry you love him.* I was shocked to hear God's prodding. I didn't feel love for Larry and I believed he had long since ceased loving me. I wasn't about to give Larry ammunition against me. After all, if he heard those three little words, "I love you," he might think I was approving of his negligence. He was always away, working at two jobs and also had a flying hobby. He was never home! So approving his behavior was the last thing I wanted to do. I flatly refused.

God gently spoke to my heart the same message a second time and I adamantly refused again! Then a third time the Holy Spirit caused a sensation in my heart but the message was a little different: *Then think it the next time you see Larry.*

I thought, *That's very strange.* But if he doesn't hear me then he can't use it against me. *Alright, Lord, I'll do it, even if it's not true.*

That evening, Larry returned from a flying trip and as he walked down the hall toward me, I stared at him, gulped, and thought, *I love you...* and then after a pause, I thought, *but I don't really.*

Then the most amazing thing began to happen. By making that ever so slight effort to love Larry, the feelings of hate dissipated and more loving feelings took over. I also came to recognized that I'd been holding Larry completely responsible for my happiness. My "all or nothing" thinking began to change as I realized that Larry couldn't meet all my needs— only God could.

God continued to work within my heart. I became convicted about my behavior of trying to control Larry and all of life.

Through prayer, reading books, Bible study, and asking other women to hold me accountable for my own growth, I began to view my situation in a different light. I had come to realize that I couldn't change Larry, I could only change myself, as I surrendered to God.

On the day I began to see myself and my situation through God's eyes, I went into the laundry room and washed off those rotting apple pieces. I no longer needed a memorial to a rotten marriage. Symbolically, I washed the rotten attitudes off my heart and mind and began to trust God with my marriage and my life.

In time, Larry noticed that I wasn't as angry and demanding of him and agreed to go on a couples retreat with me, which God used as a turning point in our marriage. That was in 1978. Today, we are best friends and the most important person in each other's life. We tell each other several times a day "I love you," and we mean it, every single time.

I'll never forget those rotting apple pieces because now I enjoy a laundry room free from them, just like my heart is free from bitterness and anger.

# HE LORD'S LULLABIES

## MELINDA LANCASTER

*As a mother comforts her child, so will I comfort you.*

ISAIAH 66:13

"LOVE COMFORTETH LIKE SUNSHINE AFTER RAIN."

*William Shakespeare*

The way that God deals with me is very interesting. Sometimes, depending on the situation, I relate to Him in my "parental role," and yet at other times, I relate in what would almost seem to be "child like."

A week after our son's first birthday, we found ourselves in the emergency room with a very ill baby boy. His condition was critical, and we were taken by ambulance to one of the Children's Hospitals in the area. It is difficult as a parent to see your child ill and to have to stand by while some things that must be done tear painfully at your heart.

We suppressed sobs more than once as he bravely endured what we knew was necessary for him to survive the crisis and recover. One of those things was a feeding tube. It was one of those things that hurts to look at…still it was a necessity for the tests and for any procedures that they needed to run on him.

Throughout the night and into the wee hours of the morning, he was pelted with one test after another. I would not leave his side for even a moment, though many times I could hear my husband sobbing out in the hallway. Those memories are deeply embedded into our minds…even to this day, but there is also something else that I heard time and time again. Each time that he was going through a test, I would find myself leaning down and singing softly in his ear. Most of the time I was simply singing, "Jesus Loves Me," to my son over and over again. It brought waves of comfort to both of us, and the nurses commented on the calming affect it had on him— not bad considering I was a first-time parent and exhausted and worried just as any parent would be. The music kept right on coming from somewhere deep inside of me, no matter what was happening or how I felt.

Just last week we celebrated our son's 13th birthday. Ironically, the tables were turned, and I was the one facing  an unpleasant procedure—the worst for me was having to endure a feeding tube for six days. One night when all my visitors had gone and I was feeling extremely restless, the Holy Spirit brought to my mind the Lord's Words in the book of Zephaniah…"He will rejoice over you with gladness, He will quiet you with His love, He will rejoice over you with singing."

Suddenly I could picture it...my Heavenly Father, not even a step away from me, gently wiping my tears, calming my fears, and all the while singing sweet lullabies of love in my ear. What a picture of the most loving and sweetest music this side of Heaven!

Today, you may be very weak with illness—physically, spiritually, or emotionally, or you may be facing many unpleasant things that bring with them great fear. Remember this, if I—as an earthly parent—could comfort my little child in his time of great need, how much more can the Almighty Father God comfort you right now? He has promised to be there in your greatest time of need, to quiet you with His love, and to be right there next to you whispering in your ear. Let Him drown out all the pain and sorrow. He will comfort you, and—if you listen quietly at this very moment—He will calm and soothe you with lullabies of love from up above.

# BCs AND SLEEPLESS NIGHTS

## MARLENE BAGNULL

*Think about all you can praise God for and be glad about.*

PHILIPPIANS 4:8 TLB

"A STATE OF MIND THAT SEES GOD IN EVERYTING IS EVIDENCE OF GROWTH IN GRACE AND A GREATEFUL HEART"

*Charles G. Finney*

Sharon, our eleven-year-old daughter, had been complaining that it hurt her to run. We assumed it was growing pains or a pulled muscle; but when several days later the pain persisted, I took her to the doctor.

"Your daughter has a slipped capital epiphysis," the doctor said to me privately after examining her.

I was frightened by the gravity of his voice. "What does that mean?" I asked anxiously.

"The ball has slipped out of her hip socket," he said as he drew a picture to illustrate what he meant. He paused as he looked up at me solemnly. "She will need to be in a body cast, perhaps for a full year."

"Oh no. No!" I couldn't imagine this happening to my

active tomboy daughter.

"I'm sorry. I really am," the doctor replied. "You may want to get another opinion from an orthopedic specialist."

He called my daughter back in and, as gently as possible, tried to explain to her what had gone wrong with her hip. I fought back tears. *Oh Lord, please help me to be strong,* I prayed silently.

I was shaking as we left the doctor's office. I had no words of comfort or reassurance for Sharon. I felt so helpless.

We were silent on the way home in the car. I knew Sharon was badly frightened, but it was obvious she was trying to be brave. There were no tears or angry "why me" questions.

I called my husband. Immediately he came home from work and together we took Sharon to another doctor. He suggested the alternative of traction and later surgery. There would still be a two-month recovery period, but he assured us that after that Sharon would again be able to run and play.

Nervously we admitted our daughter to the hospital. I was hurting so bad for her, but I still did not have any words to help ease her pain. Leaving her there that evening was one of the hardest things I ever had to do.

Sharon was in traction for the next two weeks. Each day I became more physically and emotionally exhausted from running back and forth to the hospital, trying to take care of my home and preschooler, and especially exhausted from worry. Would the surgery be successful? Would the pins they planned to put in her hip hold? How much pain would she have? How long and difficult would the recovery be?

Problems however, never seem to come just one at a time. My husband had recently started a new job after a period of unemployment. I was aware of the pressure he was under to learn something new, as well as the anxiety he was feeling as to whether the insurance would cover Sharon's hospitalization. In addition, I was in the first trimester of pregnancy. I hadn't been feeling good even before Sharon went in the hospital, but now real complications began to develop. I feared I would lose the third child we had longed for.

"I'm so worn out," I shared with a friend. "I'm exhausted when I go to bed, yet I haven't been able to sleep through the night since Sharon has been in the hospital."

"And if you aren't able to sleep at night, you'll not be able to keep coping during the day," my friend understandingly voiced my unspoken fear.

"I know, but how can I turn my mind off in order to get to sleep? I've tried praying, but even that doesn't help."

"Maybe your prayers are just a continued focus on your worries. Why not try praying thank-you prayers instead? When I found it impossible to sleep during those months when my husband was so sick, I started thanking God for something representing each letter of the alphabet. I even thanked Him for silly things that I always took for granted. Sometimes I had to go through the alphabet two times, but I did eventually fall asleep."

That night as I again tossed back and forth I remembered my friend's words.

*Lord, you know the worries that are pressing down around me. I don't have to keep telling you about them. You know also how desperately I need to get a good night's sleep. Lord, help me to look beyond all of these awful things that have been happening  and look to the many blessings I still have.*

*Thank you, Lord, for air to breathe, for my friend Carol, for daisies, for my ears, for food, green grass, my husband. Thank you for icicles, and jeans, and kangaroos...*

That time of crisis did pass. Our daughter's recovery was more difficult and lengthy than anticipated, but God gave her and us the strength we needed. He even drew us closer to Himself and to one another.

As we had feared, our insurance did not cover all of the hospital and doctor expenses, but payment schedules we could handle were arranged.

Four months after Sharon was off crutches and running and playing like before, we were blessed with a healthy baby boy.

Life is not always easy. There are times when we hurt inside and feel helpless to control the challenges facing us. But I am learning to thank the Lord for the ABC's of all His blessings. I am experiencing His peace anew in my life—bringing restful sleep to my nights and vibrant strength to my days.

# $\mathcal{N}$OT SO SMART AFTER ALL?

## PENNIE BIXLER

*Sons are a heritage from the Lord,*

*Children a reward from Him.*

PSALM 127:3 NIV

I had always wanted children. That has always been my desire. Always.

My earliest memories consist of baby dolls and the joy I had tending to them as if they were real. I named each one and made special outfits for them out of scraps of material. I felt as though God was preparing me all along to be a wonderful mother.

As a teenager, my love for children grew. I was constantly being asked to babysit for one family or another, and I threw myself into each babysitting job I took. I planned games and stories and craft projects to do with the children. And I would pretend that they were my own. I daydreamed about marrying the man of my dreams and having a houseful of children.

I was so elated the day that I found out that my husband and I were expecting our firstborn—a son. We decided I would quit working and concentrate on raising a family. I had told my boss of our plans, and he exclaimed, "What's a smart girl like you going to do at home? And with a baby?" His comment did not dampen my enthusiasm. In fact, it comforted me. If I could do such a bang-up job at work, then keeping the home fires burning was sure to prove to be a piece of cake! God could trust me with this. How could I lose? I looked forward to spending time at home—clearly the easy choice—and not having to go to work for a few years. I had not only prayed for this child but each moment of my life up until now was building toward this calling. I had planned it out in my mind how I would be the best mommy for my little boy. I would quit work and spend my days organizing and playing with my family.

The baby took his time in coming, and I was finally induced ten days after my due date. This strapping 9 lb. 4 oz. baby boy came into this world screaming. The nurse put his naked red body on my belly and he lifted his head up with his strong neck and wailed "Maaaaaaaaaaaammmm!" The doctor and his staff just laughed because it sounded incredibly like "Mom!". I never knew I could fall in love so deep.

Everything about his trip home was full of promise. We placed our new son in his new car seat, and took him to the nursery I had decorated especially for him. All of his little baby bottles were lined up on the counter and I just couldn't wait to use those cute little newborn diapers! I just knew I'd be the mother of all mothers. I was so looking forward to playing house.

It wasn't long before I was singing a different tune. *God! This is such a great responsibility! I can't do this! What have I done? I don't know how to be a mother! I'm not competent enough! I thought this would be easier!* I silently pleaded with God to turn my crazy life back around. Sleep deprived, I was trying to get my little one to sleep. Unfinished cleaning projects were evident throughout the house. My "playing house" turned into a nightmare. I felt alone and ashamed that I could not do the simple task of keeping my baby happy. It had been long days of unsuccessful attempts at holding things together on the homefront. I had never been so ill-equipped for a job in my life. I was unkept. The laundry was mounting. My new infant son never seemed to stop crying, and neither had I. I had a flashback of my boss telling me "What's a smart girl like you going to do at home with a baby?" At the time, his comment amused me. Now it haunted me. I never felt more inadequate for a job...a smart girl like me...not so smart at all.

It is now five years later. My son, Aaron, has taught me so much about selflessness and sacrifice. I have seen the world again as though it were for the first time. I have studied bugs and tadpoles. I have read countless books of trivia on dinosaurs and the solar system. His laughter has brought a new song to my heart, and opened my eyes to what truly matters in this life. His crayon drawings of dragons adorn my refrigerator and I wear the precious paperclip jewelry fashioned exclusively for me. We have spent five years taking walks in the rain, collecting autumn leaves and making snow angels. I have been the recipient of peanut butter and jelly smooches. I have spent hours in doctors' waiting rooms during the cold and flu season. We have danced and skipped five years away.

Now I try not to let him see the tears that I am holding back as he ascends the steps of the bus for his first day of school. This boy, who clung to me since birth, scrambles eagerly into the bus awaiting his ride into maturity....without ever looking back. *Wait, God!* my heart cries, *I'm not ready for this! It wasn't enough time! I cannot relinquish this great responsibility for this precious child to somebody else! They can't love him like I do.* And then a still, quiet voice answers, *He's been in My hand the whole time. I love him even more than you do. And I'll continue to watch over him. He's mine...and he's yours.  No matter what happens, that will never change."*

I turn and walk away as the tears fall down my face.  I will always be Aaron's Mommy.  I relish the treasure of every memory—every day I have spent with him instead of co-workers.  I have invested my very best and am profoundly thankful to God for the blessing Aaron has been in my life.  And I finally see that I was pretty smart all along....

# *G*IVE HIM UP

## CATHLEEN A. POULSEN

*Therefore, if anyone is in Christ, he is a new creation;*
*the old has gone, the new has come!*

2 CORINTHIANS 5:17, NIV

I looked up from the book I was reading to see my youngest son step in the front door. His eyes were cast down, his gaze not quite meeting mine. "Hey," he mumbled as he headed for the garage. I noticed a tattoo on his back, the fourth one so far, and wondered why he would choose to have a tiger permanently etched into his skin.

My heart felt like a rock inside my chest. What happened to that little boy with the shining brown eyes so full of mischief and passion for life? My husband and I had painfully watched Jed's teen years disintegrate into trouble from breaking the law, not attending classes and eventually buying and selling drugs. Now in his twenties, he no longer lived at home and rarely came by except to pick up something he had

> "FORGIVENESS IS THE ANSWER TO THE CHILD'S DREAM OF A MIRACLE BY WHICH WHAT IS BROKEN IS MADE WHOLE AGAIN, WHAT IS SOILED IS AGAIN MADE CLEAN."
>
> *Dag Hammarskjold*

stored in the garage.

We had made numerous pleas over the last two years regarding his chosen lifestyle and the change that needed to be made. It didn't take a lot of wisdom to see Jed was going to pay some heavy consequences if he didn't make different choices soon. My heart sank each time he rejected our loving proposals of help.

Within a few minutes, having retrieved what he came for, he headed back for the front door. "I love you, Jed," I whispered as my son again walked out the door.

Quietly, I breathed the same prayer I had been praying for months: *Lord Jesus, please bring Jed back to your loving arms. Open his eyes so that he may see where his life is going and turn it around.*

Several weeks passed and as the holidays approached, I thought of our family's past holiday reunions. Christmas seemed like such a ritual these days. We went through the routines of giving and receiving gifts, but love was not the center of what we were doing.

On a whim, I popped my new Don Potter CD in the player. I only listened half-heartedly as I curled my hair with the iron. My mind kept wandering back to my family and why we had drifted so far from each other. Another song came on, titled "Give Them Up." I listened to the words about wives, and husbands and children and how the Father is calling them back to Himself. Almost instinctively I began to pray *Lord, I know you are calling Jed. The world has to give him up. He belongs to You.*

Later that same evening, as we said goodbye to the last person leaving our Wednesday night small group meeting the telephone rang. It was Jed's girlfriend and I could tell she was upset. "I need to talk to you. Are you alone?" She had been driving up and down the street waiting for the cars to leave our driveway before she called. As she entered, I braced myself for the news I had been expecting for some time. "Jed has been arrested and he's in a lot of trouble," she said as she buried her face in her hands and sobbed.

My husband and I comforted her for the next half hour. We agreed that this was the best thing that could have happened to Jed. Now he would be able to think about things and while it would be painful, maybe he would make some changes. I knew I was speaking by faith and that Jed could just as easily go in the opposite direction. I had seen many others be confronted with their lives and instead of repenting and going toward God, they just hardened their hearts and turned further away from Him.

I dreaded speaking to my son in jail. I wanted to remain unemotional and not break down when I heard his voice on the phone. My husband took the first call from our wayward child, which only lasted a few minutes. I didn't speak to Jed until several days later and when I did, he said, "Mom, don't feel sorry for me. I know all of you tried to talk me out of what I was doing, but I wouldn't listen. God is working on me."

The following Wednesday, with no explanation, Jed's bond was reduced and he came home. The story he told to us about his experience in that jail still astonishes me to this day.

When he was taken to the jail, he was put in a six-hour lockdown cell. He could only pace two steps forward and two steps back. By the time he was put into a regular cell, he was feeling the Lord near. It just so happened there was a book in his cell titled "The Dynamics of Worship" by James P. Gills. He began to read it and couldn't put it down. "Everything I needed to know was in that book," he told us. "I asked God to forgive me and to show me what He wanted me to do and I would obey. I even got to talk to someone else in my cell and when I left, even though I wanted to bring the book home, I left it for him to keep reading."

Jed was at church that next Sunday and went forward to rededicate his life to Christ. I come home now to find his Bible open on his bed, or when I turn on the TV I notice it is preset on the Contemporary Christian station. He has recruited a few other guys who recently became Christians and they have formed a Christian men's fishing group with a man in the church who owns a boat. They pray before they go out and talk about life, music, and provide accountability for each other.

The other day Jed pointed to a tattoo on his right arm. It's a circle with rays of fire coming out from behind. In the circle are the letters "H.S."

"This used to stand for 'Hit Squad'," Jed told me.

"But now it stands for 'Holy Spirit.'"

# THE HARE-RAISING EAR INCIDENT: A TYPICAL HAFER FAMILY ROAD TRIP

## TODD AND JEDD HAFER

*Like a madman shooting firebrands or deadly arrows is a man*
*who deceives his neighbor and says, "I was only joking!"*

PROVERBS 27:18-19 NIV

"WHETHER ON THE ROAD OR IN AN ARGUMENT, WHEN YOU SEE RED, IT'S TIME TO STOP."

—*Jan McKeithen*

Our dad has always understood that a pastor's life can be hard on his family. That's why when we were kids, he'd load the family into our 1967 Chrysler Monstrosity and drive us to some remote spot for a little R&R. Most of you think that *R&R* stands for rest and relaxation, for us it came to mean "Retribution and Revenge."

You see, when you pack four brothers into the backseat of a car, conflicts over territorial boundaries and personal hygiene are no doubt going to emerge.

Dad handled our battles calmly. He never threatened to turn the Monstrosity around and go home, even though no one would have minded. On one fateful trip we had stopped to visit our grandparents, who lived in a retirement community inhabited by 200 elderly people and about 2,000 rabbits. We had always loved the sight of the abundant bunnies frolicking everywhere, and we loved the prospect of catching one and making it our own. But on previous trips, we had always been unsuccessful.

To our great surprise, Bradd, using knowledge he'd gleaned from Roadrunner cartoons, fashioned a crude trap that actually nabbed a fat black-and-white carrot chomper that we dubbed Mr. Spanky. To our even greater surprise, Mom and Dad agreed to let Mr. Spanky accompany us for the remainder of our trip. Most surprising of all, we were only a half mile from our grandparents' home when Mr. Spanky used the entire backseat as his own personal rest stop.

"That's it, Mr. Spanky!" Chadd screamed. "You're stew meat!"

"It's not Mr. Spanky's fault," Bradd protested. "He just got excited and went wee, wee, wee all the way ho—"

"Excited?" Chadd interrupted. "I'm excited, too! But you don't see me wetting on everyone!"

"If we make the rabbit into stew, can I have his feet for good luck?" Jedd asked.

Before things went too far, Dad stopped the car and freed Mr. Spanky who, feeling refreshed and jovial, hopped away in the direction of the retirement community.

Bradd wasn't the most popular person in the Monstrosity that day. All of us chided him mercilessly: "Hey, Bradd, maybe you can catch a skunk next time! Or how about a porcupine? They make great traveling companions!"

After enduring about fifteen minutes of this forceful rhetoric, Bradd snapped like a frozen toothpick, turning his wrath on Jedd, "Shut up, you puny germ! And move over! Your elbow is touching me!"

Perhaps crazed by the stench of rabbit wee-wee, Jedd fired back, "You move, Brer Rabbit! Better yet, why don't you get your soggy cottontail out of the car and hop off to live with your bunny friend!"

That did it. Bradd grabbed Jedd and started thumping him like a ripe cantaloupe. Jedd was in trouble and resorted to the only defense he knew. He reached up, grabbed a handful of hair, pulled Bradd's earlobe close, and bit down.

Bradd ceased his pummeling and screamed in horror. "He bit my ear off. He bit my ear off! I can feel it dangling!"

Chadd and Todd pulled Bradd's hand away from his ear, wanting to see some carnage firsthand. Jedd sat silently, wondering what happened to the piece of Juicy Fruit gum he'd been chewing.

"Oh, no!" Bradd wailed. "My ear just dropped into my hand! You're toast, Jedd! An ear for an ear! An ear for an ear!"

Dad pulled off the road and looked over the seat as Bradd slowly opened his hand to reveal a wet, grotesquely mutilated…wad of gum. It had stuck to his ear during the skirmish and actually protected him from the bite, which, we were disappointed to learn, barely left a mark.

We all laughed—even Bradd. But to this day, Jedd and Bradd aren't allowed to sit together in the backseat.

# ⟋IVING LIFE GOD'S WAY

After reading these true stories of people who experienced God's grace and power in their lives, perhaps you realize that you are at a point in your own life where you need special help from God.

Are you facing a temptation? A broken relationship? A major disappointment?

Are you ready to experience forgiveness and salvation? Encouragement and hope? Wisdom and inspiration? A miracle?

Though God's power and grace are deep and profound, receiving His help is as simple as ABC.

A—Ask: The only place to start is by asking God for help;

B—Believe: You must believe—have faith—that God can help you;

C—Confess: You must confess—admit—that you truly need God's help to receive it.

Living life God's way doesn't mean that all troubles disappear, but it does mean that there will always be Someone to turn to with all your needs. Call on Him now. For more information on how you can live God's way, visit our website at:

www.godswaybooks.com

# RIGHTS AND PERMISSIONS

# MEET THE CONTRIBUTORS

**Nancy C. Anderson** has been writing and speaking to women's groups for over twenty years. She lives near the coastline in Southern California with her husband, Ron, and their teenage son, Nick. She can be contacted at www.nancycanderson.com.

**Marlene Bagnull** is the director of the Colorado and Greater Philadelphia Christian Writers Conferences. She has been writing for thirty years.

**Pennie Bixler** is the founder and director of SAHMmies, an interdenominational Bible study and fellowship group for stay at home moms in the Eau Claire, WI area. She is wife of Mike Bixler. They have a son Aaron and a daughter Bridgette.

**Tonna Canfield** is a wife, mother, teacher, speaker, and author. She and her husband, Jeff, have been married twenty-one years. They have two daughters, Natalie and Erica. Tonna has been published in *Chicken Soup for the Mother* and *Daughter's Soul* and is currently writing a ladies' devotional book as well as a book about her own battle with depression. She may be reached at tonnacanfield@att.net.

**Joan Clayton**'s newest release is a daily devotional and is the religion columnist for her local newspaper. She has been included three times in *Who's Who Among America's Teachers*. She and her husband, Emmitt, reside in New Mexico.

**Jan Coleman** has learned to see God in every situation, and it's changed her life. As an author and speaker, she weaves her own personal lessons with Biblical insights and inspires readers to embrace life as an adventure with God. Her first book is *After the Locusts; Restoring Ruined Dreams, Reclaiming Wasted Years,* and she's busy pursuing her childhood passion to write and speak full time. She and Carl live in northern California, love to travel and fish.

**Gwendolyn Mitchell Diaz** grew up in Nigeria, West Africa with her missionary parents and is a graduate of the University of Pennsylvania. Gwen worked many years in the medical profession while she honed her writing skills and began her career as a mom. For several years she wrote a weekly newspaper column focusing on the family issues and incidents that took place as she and her husband raise their four active sons. Having published several books, including *The Adventures of Mighty Mom,* Gwen now gives much of her time to writing and speaking engagements, encouraging young women to enjoy the awesome privilege and responsibility of being a mom. She is convinced that God intended motherhood to be a blast and that, with His help, it can be.

**Wendy Dunham** is a wife, mom, inspirational writer, and a registered therapist for differently-abled children. When she's not playing with her children, gardening, or doing laundry, she can be found writing at her computer. She may be reached at wendyann@rochester.rr.com or write: 3148 Lake Rd., Brockport, NY 14420.

**Nancy B. Gibbs,** the author of four books, is a weekly religion columnist for two newspapers, a writer for *TWINS* Magazine, and a contributor to numerous books and magazines. Her stories and articles have appeared in seven *Chicken Soup for the Soul* books, *Guideposts* books, *Chocolate for Women, Women's World, Family Circle, Decision, Angels on Earth, On Mission Magazine, Happiness,* and many others. Nancy is a pastor's wife, a mother, and a grandmother. She may be reached at daiseydood@aol.com or by writing P.O. Box 53, Cordele, Georgia 31010.

**Teresa Griggs** loves to share the joy of Jesus, in her heart, through her compassionate speaking, writing, and singing ministry. Teresa's stories have appeared in *Stories of God's Abundance for a More Joyful Life, Ripples of Joy, Comfort for the Grieving Heart, Intimate Moments with God,* and *The Art of Helping.* She is a member of AWSA (Advanced Writers and Speakers Association) and a CLASS (Christian Leaders and Speakers Services) Speaker. She may be contacted at www.teresagriggs.com.

**Jedd Hafer** is a stand-up comic who has performed all over the country. A finalist in the "Tonight Show with Jay Leno Comedy Challenge," he is the two-time winner of the Colorado Young Writer's award, and his "Contests and Characters" sports humor column took top honors in a nationwide journalism contest. Jedd's day job is site director at The Children's Ark, a home for troubled teens. He and his wife, Lindsey, have two sons, Brennan and Bryce.

**Todd Hafer** is the editorial director at Hallmark, Inc. He also tackles a variety of writing assignments for newspapers and magazines. Todd has won several national and international writing awards, a few of which his children haven't colored on or used to play army. He enjoys competing in marathons and triathlons, though his favorite activity is spending time with his wife, Jody, and their four children, T.J., Jami, Taylor, and Olivia.

**Linda Henson** writes for a local newspaper and has contributed to various anthologies. She is a musician, counselor, and has taught language arts in the public school systems.

**Sharon Hinck** is developing a series of adventure fantasy novels that give encouragement to fight the daily battles of life. You may contact her at writer@mn.rr.com.

**Jennifer Johnson** lives in Lawrenceburg, Kentucky with her husband and three daughters. To write about Abba is her passion. Jennifer plans to teach middle school after completing college.

**LaRose Karr** lives in Sterling, Colorado, with her husband Larry and four children. Her work is published in the *God Allows U-Turns* book series and in several devotional guides. She is the editor of an online Christian inspirational digest, *Moonflower Ministry*. She believes her writing is a gift from God and gives Him all the glory. She enjoys speaking and ministering to women. You may contact her at rosiebay@kci.net

**Melinda Lancaster** is an author and minister who resides in Spring Hill, Tennessee, with her husband Greg and her son Gregory. She enjoys reading, music, and writing poetry.

**Kathryn Lay** is a full-time writer living in Texas with her family. She has written for *Guideposts, Christian Parenting Today, Discipleship Journal, Decision, Chicken Soup for the Mother's Soul, God Allows U-Turns,* and hundreds of others. She can be reached at rlay15@aol.com, or visit her website at http://hometown.aol.com/rlay15/index.html.

**Patricia Lorenz** is an internationally-known inspirational, art-of-living writer and speaker. She's one of the top contributors to the *Chicken Soup for the Soul* books with twenty stories in fifteen of the titles. She's the author of four books. including her two newest published by *Guideposts* Books in March, 2004: *Life's Too Short To Fold Your Underwear* and *Grab The Extinguisher, My Birthday Cake's On Fire.* Patricia raised two daughters and two sons and has had children in college every year for the past 16 years. She lives in Oak Creek, Wisconsin, and says she loves her empty nest and the freedom it allows to follow her dreams while she's still awake.

**Lena Hunt Mabra,** a freelance writer, recently retired from the field of Health and Wellness to spend time with family and pursue her writing full time. She is currently employed as a ghostwriter for a professional athlete and has an e-book and wellness program focusing on the balance of mind, body, and spirit for women.

**Karen Majoris-Garrison** is an award-winning author, whose stories appear in *Woman's World, Chicken Soup for the Soul,* and *God Allows U-Turns.* A wife and mother of two young children, Karen describes her family life as "heaven on earth." You may reach her at: innheaven@aol.com.

**Kathy Collard Miller** (www.KathyCollardMiller.com) is a popular women's conference speaker and the author of 47 books, including *Princess to Princess* and *Why Do I Put So Much Pressure On Myself and Others?*

**Susanne Scheppmann,** author and Christian speaker, resides in Nevada where she serves in her church as the Women's Ministries Director. She may be contacted at lambs yoke@aol.com.

**Laura L. Smith** lives in Oxford, Ohio, with her husband and two children. She is the author of the children's book, *Cantaloupe Trees,* as well as many short stories centered on her faith.

**Staci Stallings,** inspirational romance author, has seen the publication of numerous articles and novels in print, e-book, e-zine, and cyber-serial form. Her monthly newsletter *On Our Journey Home* brings comfort and joy to a vast audience. She lives in Amarillo, Texas, with her husband and three children. You may contact her at info@stacistallings.com.

**Gloria Cassity Stargel** is an assignment writer for *Guideposts Magazine;* a freelance writer; and author of *The Healing, One Family's Victorious Struggle With Cancer* published originally by Tyndale House Publishers. *The Healing* has been re-released in special updated edition by Bright Morning Publications. Call 1-800-888-9529 or Visit www.brightmorning.com.

**Christy Sterner** is the *God's Way* series editorial consultant and has 10 years of experience in the Christian publishing industry. She has written for many series including *Hugs* and *Chicken Soup for the Soul.*

**Nanette Thorsen-Snipes** is a freelance writer of 20 years and an award-winning author. She began writing in 1981 when her mother was terminally ill with cancer. She began with a year of humorous family columns in a local newspaper. She always had an interest in writing—a strong desire was born at that time to write from her heart.

**Betty Winslow,** an Ohio writer and school librarian, loves reading, writing, singing, and time with family, especially her granddaughter. She can be contacted at freelancer@wcnet.org.

# *T*ELL US YOUR STORY

*Can you recall a person's testimony or a time in your own
life when God touched your heart in a profound way?
Would your story encourage others to live God's Way?
Please share your story today, won't you?
God could use it to change a person's life forever.*

For Writer's Guidelines, future titles, and submission
procedures, visit:
www.godswaybooks.com

Or send a postage-paid, self-addressed envelope to:

God's Way, Editorial
6528 E. 101st Street, Suite 416
Tulsa, Oklahoma 74133-6754

This and other titles in the *God's Way* series
are available from your local bookstore.

*God's Way for Fathers*
*God's Way for Mothers*
*God's Way for Teens*
*God's Way for Women*

Visit our website at:
www.whitestonebooks.com

*"...To him who overcomes I will give some of the hidden manna to*
*eat. And I will give him a white stone,*
*and on the stone a new name written which*
*no one knows except him who receives it."*

REVELATION 2:17 NKJV

WHITE STONE BOOKS
LAKELAND, FLORIDA